THE BRITISH
4-6-0

BRITAIN'S 4-6-0 locomotives were among the most versatile and widely used types ever built. The basic ten-wheel design ranged in scope from the first humble goods engines of the Highland Railway to the Kings and Castles which handled the Great Western Railway's top expresses, from the stylish passenger engines of pre-grouping companies like the Great Eastern and the Caledonian to the utilitarian mixed-traffic designs of the LMS and LNER. Under the auspices of British Railways, 4-6-0s continued to be built right up to the end of steam locomotive construction in the 1950s and they were, in fact, the very last type of main-line engine to remain in service on the nationalised network.

JOHN CLAY is one of Britain's most distinguished locomotive historians and here he has assembled a wealth of detail to trace the development of the 4-6-0 type over the years. His text is supported by the largest selection of illustrations of British 4-6-0 locomotives ever to have been gathered together in one volume. These depict virtually all permutations of the type and, since most have never previously been published, they will form a valuable historical record for enthusiasts, modellers and students of locomotive design.

THE BRITISH
4-6-0
John F. Clay

NEW ENGLISH LIBRARY
TIMES MIRROR

Introduction

THE BRITISH 4-6-0 was a splendid locomotive. For more than seventy years it served the railways of Britian reliably and often with distinction. Many specimens are preserved, and some of them are frequently seen in steam, but the 4-6-0 has also secured a lively hold on the affectionate memories of thousands of railway enthusiasts.

A detailed history of the British 4-6-0 locomotive would require a whole series of books each larger than this: but we do not set out to present such a history. Our intention is to tell the locomotive's story in outline and to provide a background to the pictures – and, perhaps, by doing so to keep older memories fresh and to stimulate interest among people who are too young to remember the magical attraction of steam passenger trains.

We make no special pleading for the 4-6-0 type as compared with others, but we hope the qualities of 4-6-0s will emerge in proper perspective. Details of performance have been taken only from the properly confirmed records. Where horsepower is quoted, the figures are either taken from official test reports or, where calculated, are arrived at from the methods advocated by Group Captain J N C Law – who is thanked for his assistance.

Our thanks are also due to the photographers whose pictures in this book do so much to help keep the age of steam alive.

John F Clay

Leicester
March 1976

Copyright © Colourviews Ltd 1977

First published in Great Britain by New English Library, Barnard's Inn, Holborn, London EC1N 2JR in 1977.

Printed in Italy by Fratelli Spada, Ciampino, Rome.

4500 32183 (hardcover)
4500 32396 (paperback)

Front cover:
A Black Five climbing Shap with a summer Saturday extra in 1963
M POPE

Right: The last Saint to remain in service, No 2920 *Saint David* climbing towards Sapperton Tunnel on a farewell SLS special

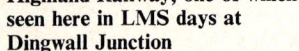

Britain's first 4-6-0 was the
Jones Big Goods of the
Highland Railway, one of which is
seen here in LMS days at
Dingwall Junction
R G JARVIS

The Old Companies' 4-6-0s

THE 4-6-0 type of locomotive was particularly well suited to British operating conditions. The high proportion of its total weight that contributed to adhesion allowed a 4-6-0 to make crisp, clean starts and to keep its feet well without slipping when climbing steep gradients in bad weather, yet retain a capacity for high-speed running. A disadvantage was the difficulty of locating an adequate ashpan owing to the position of the rear coupled axle. The presence of driving wheels under the cab tended to make 4-6-0s ride more roughly than 4-4-2 'Atlantics' or 4-6-2 'Pacifics', though other details of design made individual types exceptions to the general rule.

The world's first 4-6-0 was built in the United States in 1847 for slow, heavy freight service in a mountainous area. But by the end of the century 4-6-0s were in use over a wide range of duties in America. In 1895 a mixed-traffic 4-6-0 of the Lake Shore and Michigan Southern Railroad ran 86 miles from Erie to Buffalo in 70 min 46 sec with a maximum speed, it was said, of 92 mph. This was an astonishing performance for an engine with 5 ft 8 in driving wheels yet, in contrast to many exaggerated claims for speed by America in this period, the run seems to be well authenticated. The potential capacity for high-speed running by 4-6-0 locomotives promised well in the new century which lay ahead.

Above: The first class of 4-6-0 intended for passenger service was built for the NER in 1899. No 761 of this class was retained as a brake locomotive at the Rugby Testing Station until 1951
J M JARVIS

Left: No 36, built at Swindon, was the first 4-6-0 in England. It was intended for experimental service on the South Wales coal trains
H GORDON TIDEY

Right: No 2112 of NER class S1 built for express service passing Beningbrough with an East Coast express
H GORDON TIDEY

Although a number of 4-6-0s had been built in Britain for export, the first type for service in this country appeared in 1894. The toughest main line in the United Kingdom was the Scottish Highland Railway. There were other lines with gradients as steep, but the combination of length and inclination made the Highland especially difficult in winter when the elements as well as gravity had to be overcome. In 1894, David Jones built his 'Big Goods' 4-6-0, the largest and most powerful locomotive in the country at that time. Although they were intended for goods traffic, the Jones 4-6-0s ran many miles of useful service as pilots, or in charge of holiday extras when passenger traffic was heavy. It is good to know that one of these historic engines has been preserved in Glasgow.

South of the border, the 4-6-0 first appeared on the Great Western in 1896 when William Dean built No 36 – an experimental freight engine with the inside cylinders and outside frames typical of Dean's designs – for the heavy South Wales traffic. In 1899 there followed No 2601, the first of the 'Krugers', which was based on No 36 but had domeless boilers that showed the influence of G J Churchward, the second in command at Swindon. No 2601 was a 4-6-0 but the remainder of the class were 2-6-0s and it was as 2-6-0s that the class was developed. Churchward was to play a large part in the future of the 4-6-0.

The Highland Railway might easily have been the first to introduce a 4-6-0 passenger engine, as David Jones was working on such a design, based on his goods 4-6-0, at the time of his enforced retirement following an accident. His successor modified some details and the engine finally appeared in 1900 as Peter Drummond's 'Castle' class, but by that time a passenger 4-6-0 had been built by Wilson Worsdell for the North Eastern. Both the Highland and North Eastern engines had two outside cylinders and driving wheels of relatively moderate diameter. Engines of the same basic type were destined to be the most numerous 4-6-0s, and the final designs for those built half a century later were similar in conception, though naturally more sophisticated in detail. The Scottish engines were intended to cope with hard slogging up mountain grades. On the NER, 4-6-0s at first ran trips on East Coast expresses, but they never seriously challenged the four-coupled engines on these trains and they were soon relegated to fast goods and excursion work. In 1901, however, Wilson Worsdell built five express engines with 6 ft 8¼ in driving wheels and with these engines the British 4-6-0 may be said to have attained full express passenger status. The large-wheeled NER 4-6-0s of Class S1 soon proved that six coupled wheels were no hindrance to fast running and, although no more were built, the late Charles Rous Marten, the leading train timing expert of his day, compared their running favourably with the later and larger NER Atlantic-type engines.

In the early years of the twentieth century 4-6-0 locomotives appeared on a number of railways but it was some time before the type was universally accepted as a high-speed express engine. In 1900 the 4-2-2 single was still performing a good deal of fast main line work especially on the GNR, the Midland and the GWR. Some designers thought that the 4-4-2 Atlantic type was the logical successor to the single. They claimed that it needed less power to move itself and there was more room for an adequate ashpan than on the 4-6-0. Opinion was divided for many years.

Above: The prototype Churchward 2-cylinder express passenger 4-6-0,
No 100 *William Dean*, shown here with taper boiler
COLOURVIEWS PICTURE LIBRARY

Below: *Duncraig Castle*, one of P Drummond's express engines
developed from plans started by D Jones, shown here as LMS No 14884
R G JARVIS

There can be little doubt that G J Churchward was the greatest British locomotive designer of the twentieth century and much of the secret of his success lay in his willingness to learn from others. He took the best features of designs in America and on the Continent and grafted them on to engines of his own which were well suited to the needs of his own railway. In 1902 he built No 100, an express 4-6-0 with two outside cylinders and a domeless boiler. The new engine created something of a sensation by its bold external lines which showed that some of its inspiration came from American practice. Later it was named *William Dean* after his predecessor. In 1903 another experimental 4-6-0 appeared, No 98, which had a taper boiler – a further adaptation of American practice.

At this time the de Glehn compound Atlantics of the Northern Railway of France were earning themselves a well-deserved reputation. Anxious to test all that was best in world practice, Churchward bought one for service on the GWR in 1903. It was No 102 *La France* and in 1905 it was joined by *President* and *Alliance*, rather larger Atlantics of the type used on the Paris-Orleans Railway. Churchward was by no means certain of the suitability of compounding for British operating conditions and he thought that his own two-cylinder simple locomotives with large diameter, long lap, long travel valves and direct steam and exhaust passages would prove to be equally efficient and more reliable in everyday service. To make the comparison fair in every way, No 171, a new 4-6-0 similar to No 98 but with 225 lb sq in boiler pressure, was converted to the Atlantic wheel arrangement. It was then possible to test, under normal operating

conditions ,the comparative merits of simple *versus* compound propulsion and the 4-4-2 *versus* the 4-6-0 wheel arrangement. Early tests soon convinced Churchward that his own simple engines were the equals of the compounds in power, speed and economy, and subsequent experience, over a number of years, showed that the simple engines had lower maintenance costs and that 4-6-0s were just as fast as Atlantics.

Although unconvinced of the value of compounding, Churchward was impressed by the easy riding of the four-cylinder compounds as compared with his own engines which were affected by the powerful thrusts of their two large outside cylinders with their 30 in piston strokes. He built a four-cylinder simple Atlantic, No 40, later named *North Star*, which incorporated the de Glehn pattern of divided drive with the outside cylinders driving the middle pair of wheels and the inside cylinders driving the leading pair. This engine appeared in 1906 and in three years it was converted to a 4-6-0, by which time there were many similar four-cylinder 4-6-0s known collectively as the Stars. Various batches were named after Stars, Knights, Kings, Queens, Princes, Princesses and Abbeys. The final Abbeys were completed in 1922/3 after Churchward had retired. The Kings were renamed Monarchs when C B Collett built the larger King class in 1927. The earlier two-cylinder 4-6-0s were known collectively as the Saints and were named after Ladies, Saints and Courts to which were added some miscellaneous names, including some from the works of Sir Walter Scott. The last Swindon Atlantic was rebuilt as a 4-6-0 in 1913, thus leaving the three French compounds as the only 4-4-2s on the line. The Courts were built with superheaters in 1911/12 and the remainder of the class was altered to conform. By the end of 1913 both the Saints and Stars were all superheated and slightly larger cylinders were standardised.

Above left: No 2906 *Lady of Lynn*, **one of the earlier Churchward 4-6-0s**
W J REYNOLDS

Above: No 2931 *Arlington Court*, **one of the later engines of the Saint class shown on the Swindon test plant**
C F OLDHAM

Left: No 4059 *Princess Patricia* **in BR days with high-sided tender working a stopping train**
P M ALEXANDER

Both two-cylinder and four-cylinder GWR 4-6-0s had the same boiler and there was little difference in power, speed and economy. By all accounts, drivers considered a Saint better when faced with hard slogging in unfavourable conditions, but the easier riding of the four-cylinder engines at high speed was appreciated. The Stars tended in time to dominate the crack expresses such as the *Cornish Riviera Limited.* The standard of basic thermo-dynamic performance reached by the Churchward 4-6-0s was never greatly improved in later designs. Progress mainly took the form of adapting their basic merit to larger designs and fitting later engines for changed operating conditions. Both Stars and Saints showed their ability to work loads of 500 tons on fast schedules and both could achieve Churchward's target of a draw-bar pull of two tons at 70 mph. At a time when it was considered quite good for a British express engine to burn between $4\frac{1}{2}$ and 5 lb of coal per dbhp/hr, the Churchward engines needed only 3 to $3\frac{1}{2}$ lb. The Swindon engines were sound in their mechanical details and GWR standards of maintenance were high. The main criticism that may, with justice, be directed against the Churchward 4-6-0s was the very meagre shelter given by their cabs.

Above: No 4066 *Malvern Abbey*,
one of the last batch of
4-cylinder Stars, photographed
in Sonning Cutting with an up
Birmingham fast train
M W EARLEY

Right: No 4005 *Polar Star* on
test on the LNWR main line in
1910
H GORDON TIDEY

Far right top: NER Class S2
mixed-traffic 4-6-0 No 815 at
York
T G HEPBURN

Far right centre: No 1099 of the
GCR Immingham class at
Nottingham Victoria
T G HEPBURN

Far right: Former GCR fast
goods 4-6-0 No 6110 at Trafford
Park shed
P M ALEXANDER

No other class of British 4-6-0 built during the first two decades of the twentieth century matched the overall performance of the Churchward engines. A number of designers also used two outside cylinders. James Manson on the Glasgow and South Western built his first 4-6-0s in 1903. These had a reputation, shared by a number of saturated contemporary 4-6-0s, 4-4-2s and 4-4-0s, of being fast downhill but not over vigorous uphill, but the final pair of superheated G&SWR 4-6-0s Nos 128/9 were very good engines for their size. The first GCR 4-6-0s built by J G Robinson for the Great Central were mixed-traffic engines intended mainly for the fish trains from Grimsby, and the same general pattern with two outside cylinders was used on several GCR classes intended for express passenger, mixed-traffic and fast goods trains. The NER built an enlarged version of their two-cylinder 4-6-0s for mixed traffic but they standardised the Atlantic for fast express work.

The two-cylinder 4-6-0 with inside cylinders, first introduced but then abandoned by the GWR, was continued in 1902 by J F McIntosh on the Caledonian with the '55' class of small-wheeled 4-6-0s especially intended for the steep grades of the Oban road, where they gave many years of good service. These were followed in 1903 by Nos 49/50, large-wheeled express locomotives still with inside cylinders. The designer's intention was to reduce double heading on the West Coast expresses between Glasgow and Carlisle. In 1906 he followed these with a larger boilered version known as the '903' or 'Cardean' class. *Cardean* became famous for its long period of reliable service on the 2 pm 'Corridor' from Glasgow to Carlisle, returning with the down train. In 1909, *Cardean* ran trials over the LNWR main line from Carlisle to Preston and on one southbound run, flogged mercilessly uphill with a 390-ton train, averaged 44 mph for 18 min on grades rising mainly at 1 in 125. This involved an indicated hp calculated at slightly over 1,500, and this was certainly a record for an inside-cylinder 4-6-0. There is no

Top left: G&SWR 4-6-0 No 129 with superheater and feed water heater, thought by many to have been the best of all G&SWR 4-6-0s
REAL PHOTOGRAPHS

Below left: One of the earlier saturated, flat-valve G&SWR 4-6-0s as LMS No 14671 at Glasgow St Enoch station
T G HEPBURN

Bottom: No 903 *Cardean*, the most famous of all Caledonian 4-6-0s

Right: No 916, one of the CR mixed traffic 4-6-0s
H GORDON TIDEY

C R

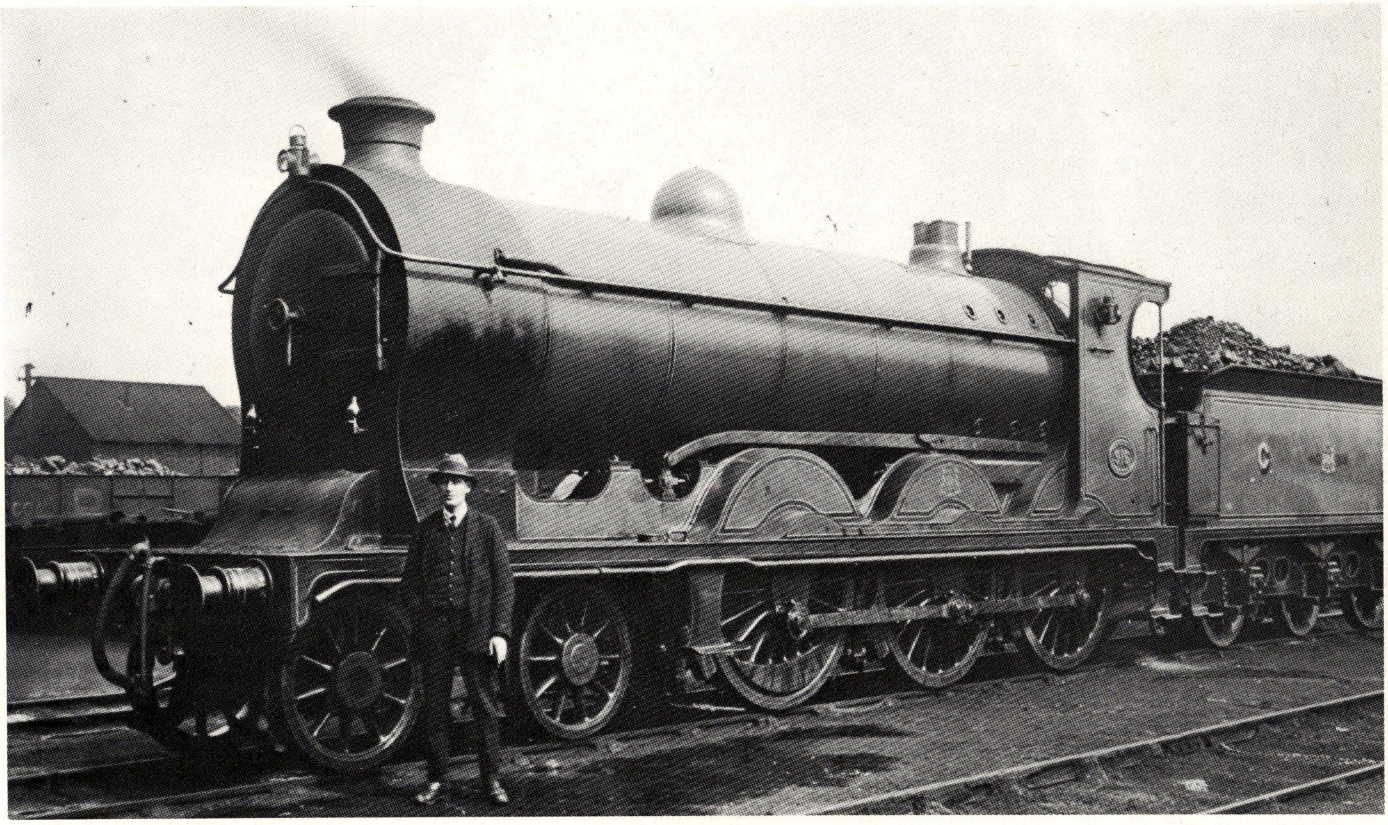

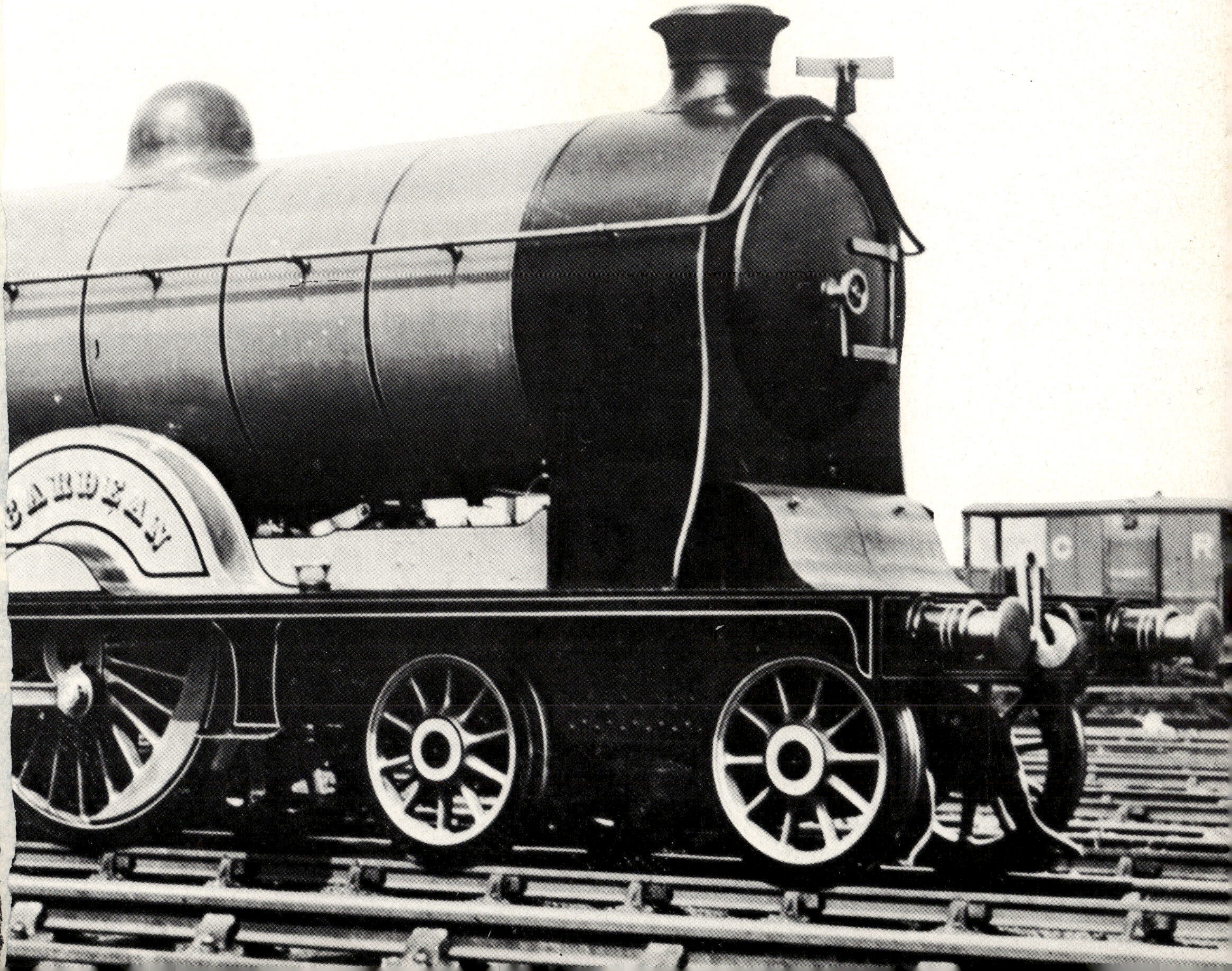
CARDEAN
C R

record of anything higher at a comparable speed even by a GWR Star or Saint, but the Swindon engines far outclassed *Cardean* in the higher speed ranges. The Caledonian built inside-cylinder 4-6-0s for freight and mixed-traffic duties.

The first 4-6-0s on the LNWR were some four-cylinder compounds built by F W Webb for mixed-traffic work in 1902. These were officially known as the '1400' class and unofficially as the 'Bill Baileys'. It is difficult to find anything good to say about them. In 1904 G Whale built the simple inside-cylinder 4-6-0s of the 'Experiment' class mainly for service over the Crewe-Carlisle section. They proved to be less consistent in their running than the corresponding 4-4-0s of the Precursor class, but in the same trials as *Cardean* an Experiment, No 2630 *Buffalo*, was given the same ruthless treatment with the result that it produced 1,280 ihp as compared with the 1,500 of the larger Scottish engine. The Experiments were followed by a similar engine for fast goods and mixed-traffic work known as the '19 in Goods' of the '285' class. In 1911 Whale's successor, C J Bowen Cooke, built the 'Prince of Wales' class – a superheated version of the Experiments. While these engines never surpassed the best work of the corresponding superheated 4-4-0s of the 'George the Fifth' class they had a wider route availability and proved to be so useful as general purpose engines that they reached a class total of 245 engines.

Although *Cardean* achieved the highest horsepower output for a British inside-cylinder 4-6-0, the largest examples of the type were the 'Sir Sam Fay' class on the GCR built in 1913. These were fine-looking locomotives but they never matched the GCR Atlantics or 'Director' class 4-4-0s in performance. They were followed by a mixed-traffic version known as the 'Glenalmond' class. Perhaps the most successful class of inside-cylinder 4-6-0s was the '1500' class of the Great Eastern. These engines were built to fit a line with very rigid weight limitations and, although relatively small, they did excellent work on the heavy 'Continental Boat Trains' from Liverpool Street to Harwich.

It has been said that the only really successful four-cylinder 4-6-0s were those of the GWR, but the LNWR could certainly claim a near miss. In 1909/10 C J Bowen Cooke organised a series of interchange trials between the LNWR and other railways. Among the visitors was the GWR No 4005 *Polar Star*. The GWR locomotive created a good impression by the quiet way in which it mastered its work. Bowen Cooke, however, shrank from the use of a boiler pressure as high as 225 lb sq in and in 1913 he produced his own design of four-cylinder 4-6-0s known as the 'Claughton' class. These engines used steam at a lower pressure but with more superheat than the Stars. The four cylinders all drove on the leading coupled axle, and this gave even better balancing than the divided drive of Churchward's 4-6-0s. The original intention was to use a bigger boiler, but this was prevented by weight restrictions and the boiler actually used had a large firebox for its size.

The Claughtons fell short of greatness. At times there were brilliant individual performances, but the average everyday standard was far lower. There were a number of defects in the design which made the engines expensive to maintain. On its day a Claughton could match the best power outputs of a GWR Star or Saint but such days were rare and, if consistency and economy were also considered, the superiority of Swindon had to be acknowledged.

A four-cylinder 4-6-0 was introduced on the Lancashire and Yorkshire Railway in 1908. As originally built, with flat valves and without superheaters, these Hughes 4-6-0s were undistinguished performers. In 1920 one was rebuilt with a superheated boiler and piston valves. The result was a sensational improvement and superheated Hughes 'Dreadnoughts' were destined to play their part in the early days of the LMS.

Below: LNWR Experiment class 4-6-0 No 1709 *Princess May*
BRITISH RAIL

Top right: GCR No 5427 *City of London* passing Belgrave and Bistall with a down express
A W FLOWERS

Below right: B17 No 2856 *Leeds United* of the 'Football Club' series at Neasden in 1936
JOHN ADAMS

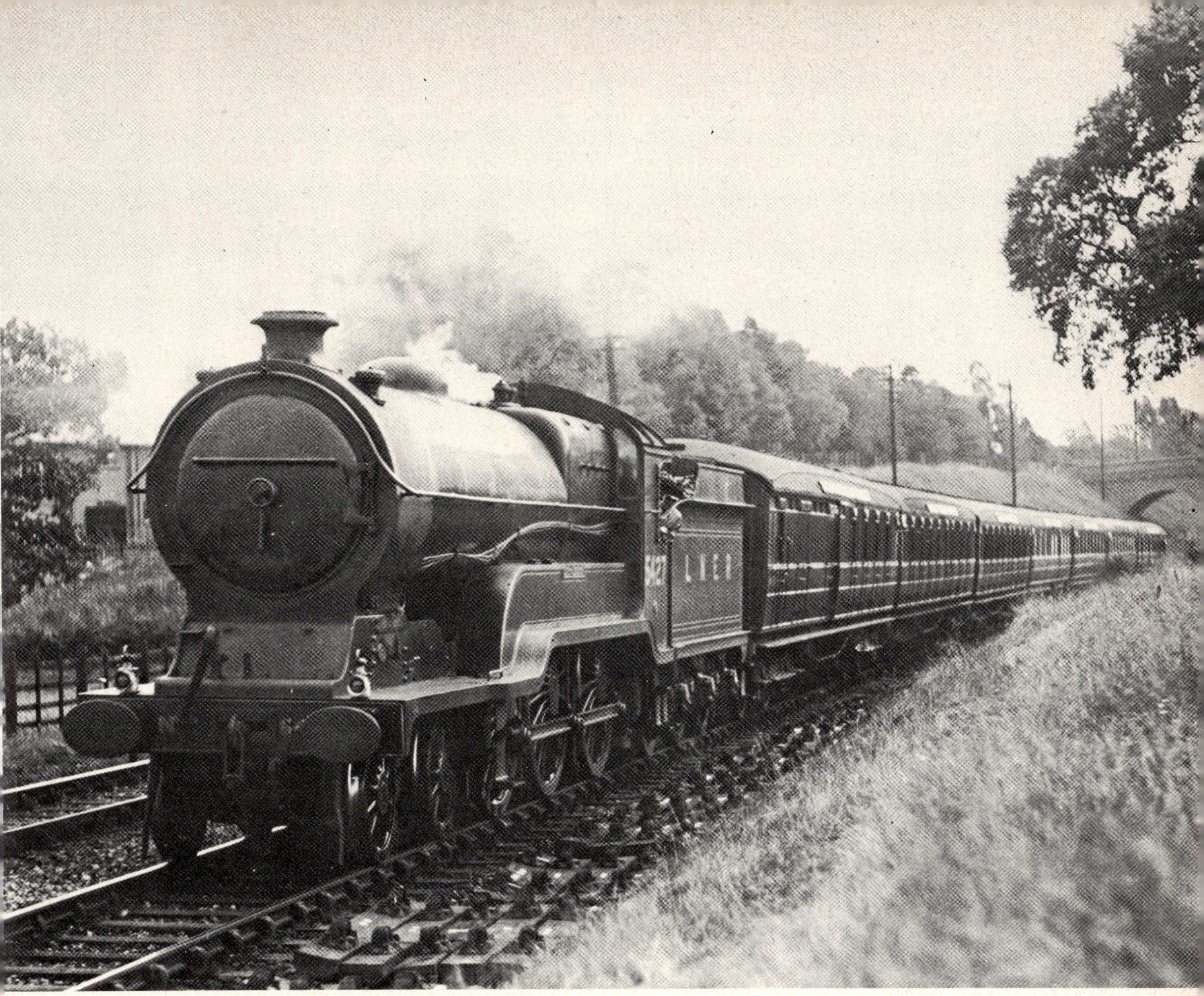
5427
L N E R

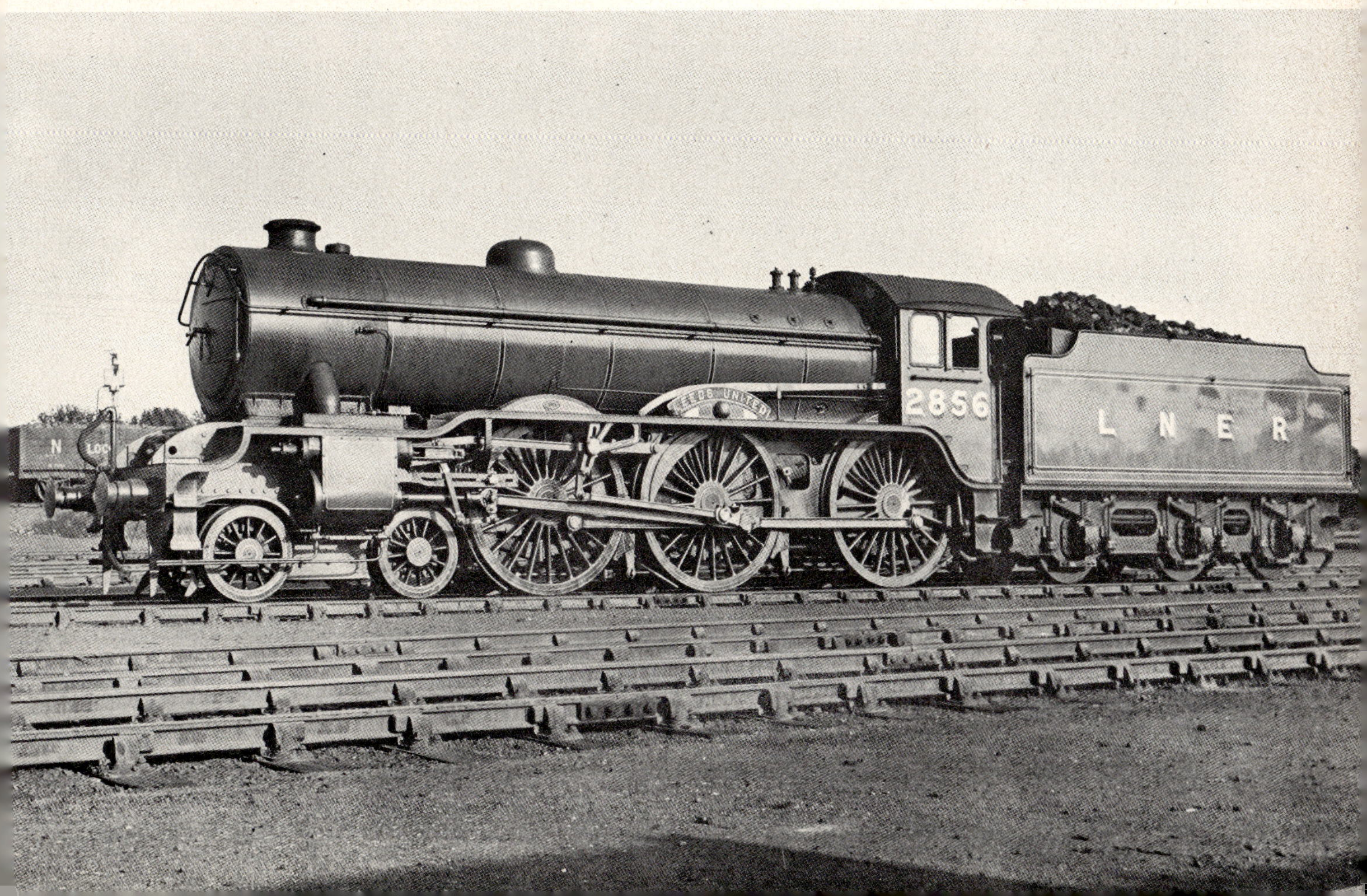
LEEDS UNITED
2856
L N E R

Top far left: GCR Sir Sam Fay class 4-6-0 No 428 *City of Liverpool* at Nottingham Victoria station in early LNER days
T G HEPBURN

Centre far left: No 25726, one of the five Princes fitted with outside Walschaerts valve gear. These engines were nicknamed 'Tishies'

Below far left: No 8753 of the 19in Goods class mixed-traffic class at Rugby
T G HEPBURN

Left: Experiment class No 5525 *Byzantium* near Nuneaton on a down semi-fast
P B WHITEHOUSE

Below: Prince of Wales class 4-6-0 No 2359 *Hermione* tackles an express train with the bustling energy typical of the LNWR

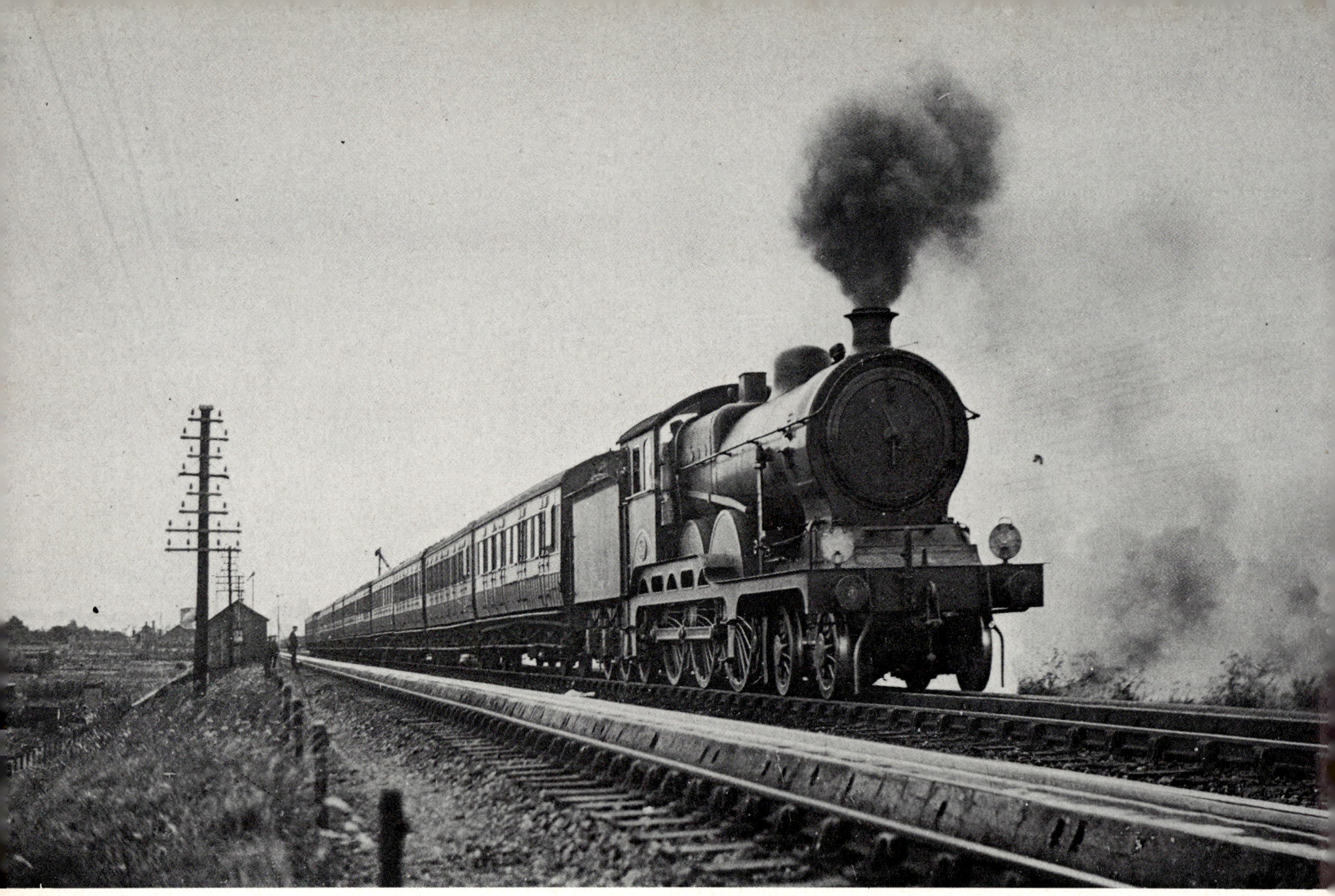

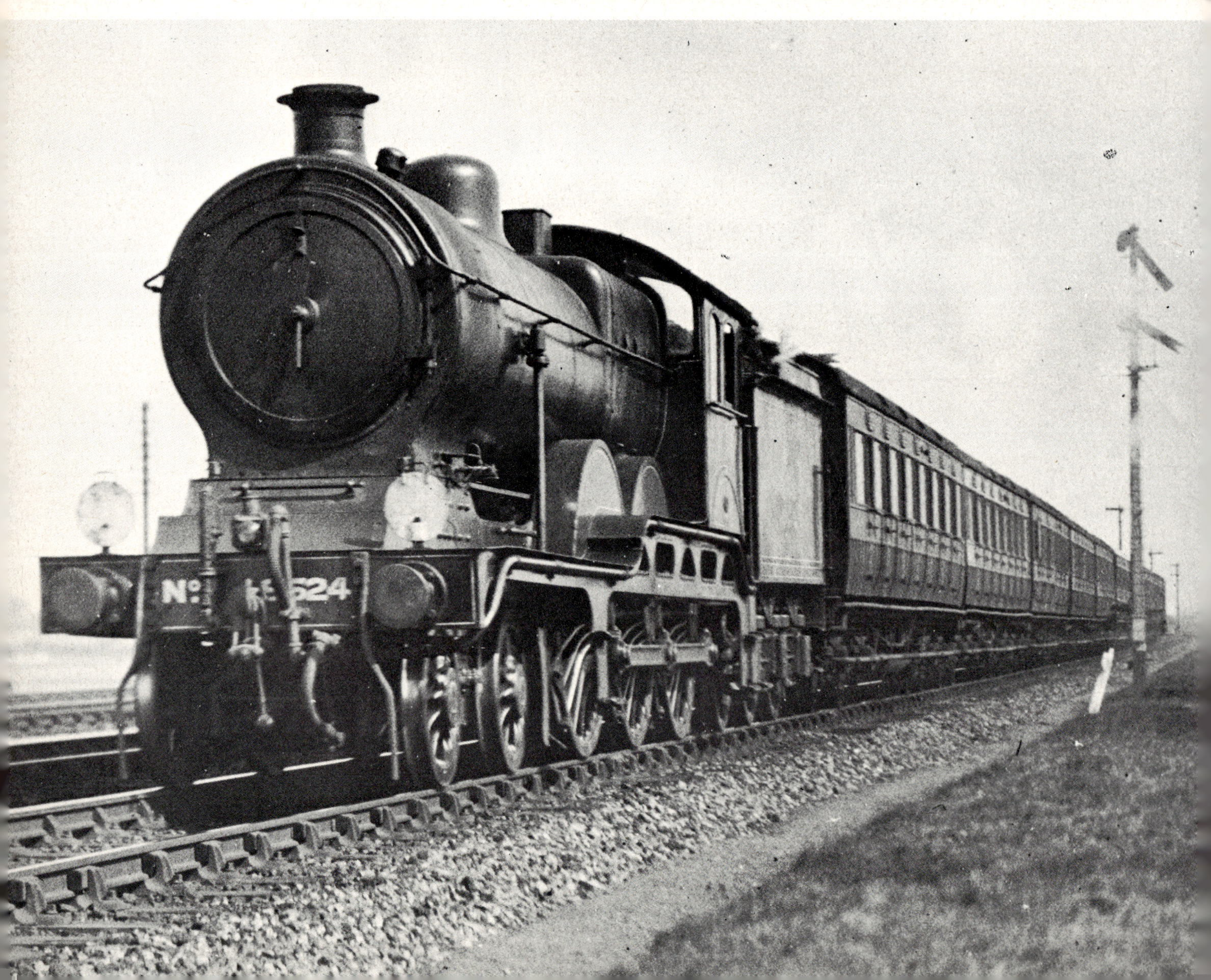

No.

One of the great locomotive designers of the nineteenth century was Dugald Drummond, who built some very successful 4-4-0s for the North British, the Caledonian, and the London and South Western Railways. He did not, however, achieve the same success with the four-cylinder 4-6-0s he built for the LSWR. The first of these appeared in 1904 and proved to be sluggish and unreliable. Nevertheless, Drummond persisted with four-cylinder 4-6-0s with relatively small driving wheels for the Salisbury-Exeter road and built a number of uniformly unsuccessful classes. In 1910 he built some with larger wheels for the expresses on easier grades such as the Bournemouth line. These were impressive engines with large splashers over their driving wheels which gave them the nickname of the 'Paddleboxes'. They were slightly better in performance and they survived in a rebuilt form into BR ownership, but nothing that they did could not have been equalled by some of Drummond's very good 4-4-0s.

Perhaps the most impressive looking four-cylinder 4-6-0s were those of the GCR, the first of which was introduced for express passenger service in 1917. They had the same boiler as the Sir Sam Fay class but they too never surpassed the best performances of the Atlantics or Directors in everyday running. A similar class with smaller wheels for mixed-traffic work followed in 1921. All these engines had a reputation for heavy coal consumption but their drivers appreciated their good riding qualities.

The three-cylinder 4-6-0 was not built in large numbers before the grouping, but it was a type destined to find fame later on. In 1919 Sir Vincent Raven built some mixed-traffic engines for the NER which were big powerful machines with a reputation for a lusty appetite for coal similar to that of the four-cylinder GCR machines. A design that might have been really outstanding proved to be most disappointing of all. These were the four three-cylinder 4-6-0s of the '956' class built in 1921 by W Pickersgill for the Caledonian main line. This was a bold design large enough to meet the most exacting demands, but the arrangement of valve gear, by which two sets of gear worked three sets of valves, proved to be unreliable in service. The engines never performed

Above left: GER No 1513 at the head of an express on Ipswich water troughs
J F CLAY COLLECTION

Below left: GER 4-6-0 as LNER B12 class No 8524 at the head of a GER express

Above: D Drummond E14 No 335 built for the Salisbury-Exeter main line
LOCOMOTIVE PUBLISHING CO

Below: Drummond class T14 large-wheeled 4-cylinder 4-6-0 No 447 fitted with steam drier and firebox water tubes
H GORDON TIDEY

work worthy of their size and they were soon relegated to fast goods and secondary work.

Pickersgill had built some outside-cylinder, two-cylinder 4-6-0s in 1916/17 and these took over some of the duties from the Cardeans. They were known as the '60' class and, although light on repair costs, did little running of any note. Similarly the '191' class built for the Oban line were disappointing – the use of an unsuperheated boiler and flat valves was unenterprising for 1922.

Perhaps the best of the later 4-6-0s to run on the Caledonian were six outside-cylinder 4-6-0s built by F G Smith for the Highland, where they were to have been known as the 'River' class. Unfortunately they were rejected by the Civil Engineer and their layout redesigned. The unacceptable engines were bought by the Caledonian who used them mainly on fast goods trains. On the Highland the unfortunate Mr Smith was followed by C Cummings who in 1918 built the 'Clan' class of outside-cylindered 4-6-0s. These proved to be sturdy hill climbers and gave good service for many years. They were followed by a smaller-wheeled version known as the Clan Goods.

On the LSWR Drummond was followed by another Scottish engineer, R W Urie, who replaced the four-cylinder 4-6-0s by strong, simple engines with two outside cylinders. The first class was the H15 mixed-traffic engines, which did some useful work on troop trains in both wars. Five of these were rebuilds from Drummond's first class of four-cylinder 4-6-0s. After the war, Urie built the N15s, with larger driving wheels for express passenger trains, and the S15, with smaller wheels for fast goods trains. The Urie 4-6-0s gave a steady, reliable performance which was not, however, brilliant.

The stock of 4-6-0 locomotives taken over by the new railway groups in 1923 was of variable quality. The best of them, the GWR Stars and Saints, could and did reach 1,500 ihp in ordinary commercial service. The Claughtons reached similar power output on test runs and occasionally approached it in ordinary service. In a thunderous all-out attack on Shap the Caledonian *Cardean* also did so but few of the other 4-6-0s ever had to exceed the 1,200 ihp attained by some of the best 4-4-0s. The Churchward engines had, however, given a startling vista of what might be expected of well-designed 4-6-0s and the grouping era was destined to see some exciting happenings.

Above: T14 No 461 at Waterloo as rebuilt by Urie with Eastleigh superheater and with firebox water tubes removed A W FLOWERS

Above right: A Hughes 4-cylinder 4-6-0 of the L&Y in original saturated condition. No 1515 heads a Manchester-Blackpool express
H GORDON TIDEY

Right: Former LNWR Claughton class 4-6-0 as LMS No 5961 on an up main-line express
H GORDON TIDEY

Left: Claughton No 5932 *Sir Thomas Williams* with tender from an ex-ROD GCR-type 2-8-0

Right: Un-named Claughton No 1092, still in LNWR livery, heads a train of Midland stock on the LNWR main line

Below: The war memorial GCR 4-cylinder 4-6-0 *Valour* passing the very tall distant signal in Saltersford Cutting near Grantham with an up express
W LESLIE GOOD

Above: GCR-type 4-cylinder mixed-traffic 4-6-0 No 5479 at Neasden shed in 1934 JOHN ADAMS

Right: No 6166 *Earl Haig* with Caprotti valve gear at Nottingham Victoria T G HEPBURN

Far right: Urie N15 class express engine No 741 H GORDON TIDEY

Top: Urie H15 2-cylinder 4-6-0 No 30490 on an Eastleigh to Salisbury empty stock train
P M ALEXANDER

Above: Urie S15 fast goods engine No 30496 on an up freight train at Reading General
P H WELLS

Right: NER S3 (LNER B16) No 61442 passing Crimple Junction near Harrogate in 1950
P M ALEXANDER

Above: A Caledonian Pickersgill 956 class 3-cylinder 4-6-0 at Perth.
These were the largest Scottish 4-6-0s
T G HEPBURN

Below: Pickersgill 60 class 4-6-0, in LMS livery, numbered 14648

Above: One of the former Highland Railway River class 4-6-0s which were sold to the Caledonian, shown here as No 14756 of the LMS. Some of these engines were later to return to the Highland line
R G JARVIS

Below: Ex-Highland Railway 4-6-0 as LMS No 14765 *Clan Stewart* at Inverness in 1934
R G JARVIS

Above: Ex-Highland Railway Clan Goods No 17956 stationed at Dingwall for service on the Kyle line in 1936
R G JARVIS

Below right: No 5005 *Manorbier Castle* with experimental streamlining at Old Oak Common shed in 1935
JOHN ADAMS

Below: GWR No 4079 *Pendennis Castle* leaving Kings Cross on a stopping train while the crew are learning the road for test running later in the week in April 1925
J F CLAY COLLECTION

The Grouping Era

WHEN peace returned after the First World War there were soon clear signs that the comfortable world in which the railways had prospered had gone for ever. Costs were rising and road competition was already so affecting railway receipts that some companies were facing bankruptcy. The inevitable decision was taken to merge the old companies into four large groups, so that the weaker concerns could be sheltered by the stronger; but, as with similar amalgamations in other walks of business life, inner rivalries hindered progress.

The grouping of 1923 found the 4-6-0 well established but the challenge of the Pacific lay just ahead. The GWR had built the first experimental Pacific in 1908 and although this solitary engine, *The Great Bear*, held a place in the affections of enthusiasts, it was never a serious rival to the Stars and Saints in everyday performance. Its size and weight limited it to the London-Bristol main line. In 1922 H N (later Sir Nigel) Gresley built a Pacific for the Great Northern and this was followed shortly by one designed by Sir Vincent Raven for the North Eastern. These East Coast Pacifics were different from *The Great Bear* in that they were intended to be prototypes for new classes to relieve hard-worked Atlantics rather than experimental exercises.

The eyes of interested observers turned towards Swindon to see if an answer was to come to the East Coast challenge. The GWR had been proud to claim that *The Great Bear* was Britain's largest and most powerful locomotive and they were unhappy to see it dethroned. The reply from Swindon came in August 1923 when it was announced that the new *Caerphilly Castle*, the first of a new class, was 'Britain's Most Powerful Express Locomotive'. When a photograph was published many people were surprised to see a 4-6-0 not much larger than the existing Star class. The 'most powerful' claim was made on the dubious basis of tractive

effort which took no account of the ability of the boiler to make the nominal figure effective under all conditions. The everyday performance of the new 'Castles' soon suggested that the claim was well justified but tractive effort was not the reason.

A GWR Castle and a Gresley Pacific were exhibited side by side at the British Empire Exhibition at Wembley in 1924 and the LNER was not amused by the GWR placard which declared that their relatively small 4-6-0 was 'Britain's Most Powerful Express Passenger Locomotive', and the suggestion that boiler size rather than tractive effort was the criterion of power. It is not intended here to become enmeshed in controversy about just what happened in the corridors of railway power, but we may examine the exchange running between a Castle and a Pacific which began in April 1925. The smaller Castle class engine handled the Kings Cross-Doncaster trains with comparative ease and impressed everyone by its quick starts from Kings Cross to Finsbury Park. The Gresley Pacific ran quite well on the GWR non-stop to Plymouth but, both on its own road and on the GWR, it burnt more coal than its 4-6-0 rival. The hearts of Swindon supporters were high that summer, but the East Coast had

Above: The pioneer Castle No 4073 *Caerphilly Castle* on a stopping train in BR days. The engine has a shorter chimney and a larger tender than when first built
P M ALEXANDER

some satisfaction during the coal strike of 1926 when the wide-fireboxed Pacifics found low-grade imported coal more digestible than did their more refined GWR rivals. Then, valves and valve gear modified from 1927 onwards as a result of the trials transformed the Gresley Pacifics.

The real reason for the Swindon triumph lay in the more efficient valve and front end design of their engine. The issue was, however, clouded by arguments over wide or narrow fireboxes, three or four cylinders, high or low pressure boilers and the Pacific or 4-6-0 wheel arrangements. At this time R E L Maunsell of the Southern was intending to build a large, express locomotive. As a stop gap he had improved the Urie N15 two-cylinder 4-6-0 design by using modern valve events and front end design. These new 4-6-0s were given names associated with the King Arthur legends and this proved to be good publicity for a sound reliable engine. No 777 *Sir Lamiel* was credited with a 83.8 mile run up from Salisbury in 72 min 41 sec with 345 tons. A fast goods version followed and the better front end made these engines faster in service than the earlier Urie mixed-traffic 4-6-0s with larger driving wheels.

Maunsell was, however, aiming at something more powerful and a large 4-6-0 with four cylinders, No 850 *Lord Nelson*, the first of the class, emerged from Eastleigh works in August 1926. The GWR had pressed the claims of tractive effort as the qualification of power and they could hardly grumble when the Southern claimed the 'most powerful' express locomotive on the grounds that their *Lord Nelson* had a tractive effort slightly higher than a Castle. It was not until 1938, however, when the Lord Nelsons had been modified by O V S Bulleid, formerly assistant to Sir Nigel Gresley at Doncaster, that they performed everyday work comparable with that of the Castles. The most obvious of the Bulleid alterations was the fitting of the Lamaitre multi-jet blast pipe and large diameter chimney. The improved Lord Nelsons had only a short time to show their powers before war broke out and after the war Bulleid built Pacifics for the heaviest duties. The Lamaitre blast pipe was also fitted to some of the Urie N15 4-6-0s, but they were never quite as reliable steamers as the later King Arthurs.

Above: No 5025 *Chirk Castle* **of the 1934 batch at the head of the** *Merchant Venturer*
P M ALEXANDER

Below: No 7033 *Hartlebury Castle,* **one of the last batch built in 1950 running in on a stopping train**
P M ALEXANDER

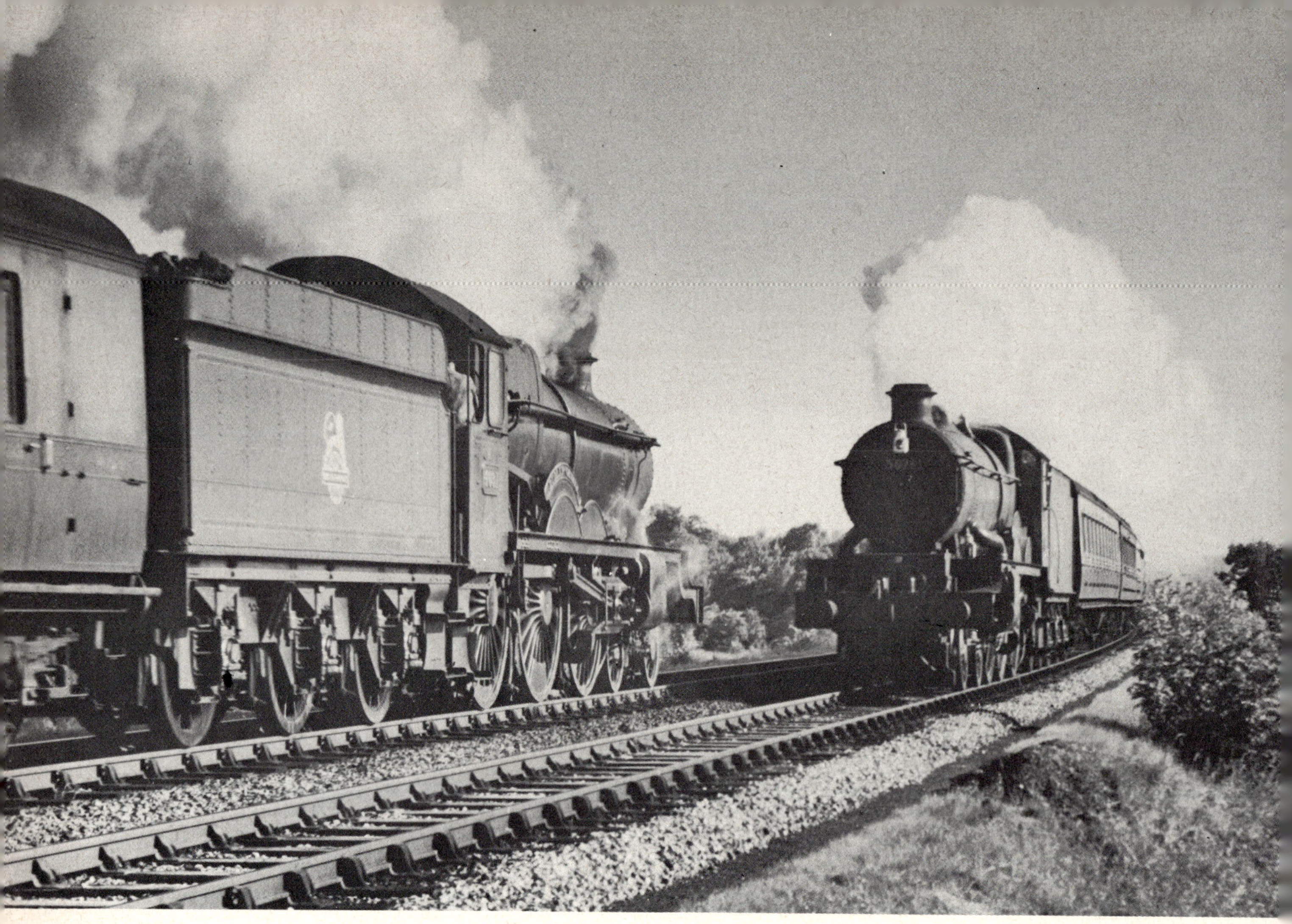

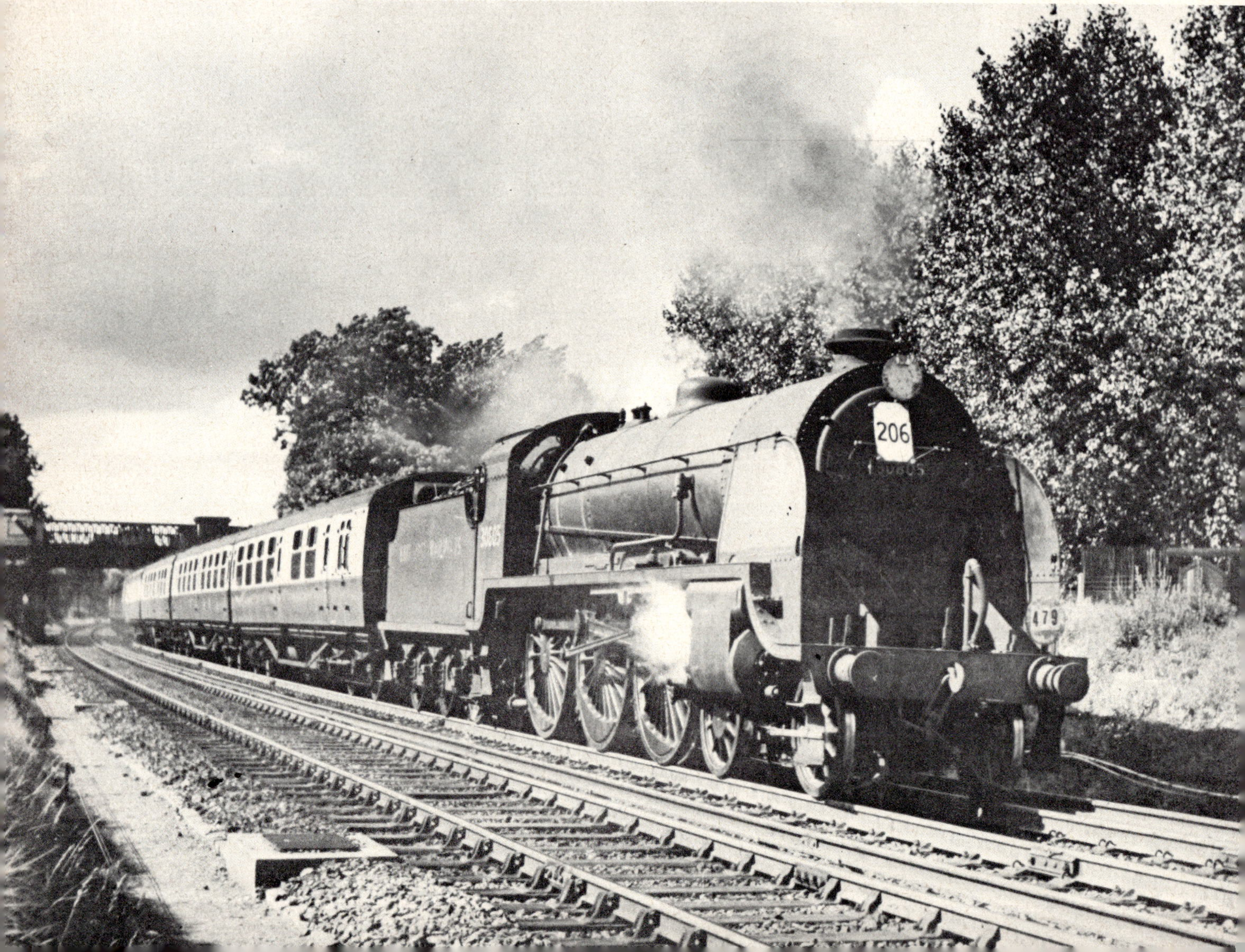
206
479

Left: A scene typical of the GWR in the steam age. Castle No 4091 *Dudley Castle* on up express passes No 5076 *Gladiator* on down stopping train
P M ALEXANDER

Below left: Maunsell King Arthur class 4-6-0 based on the Urie N15. No 30805 *Sir Constantine* with small tender for use on the SECR climbing towards Penge Tunnel with the down *Granville Express*
P M ALEXANDER

Right: Maunsell S15 fast goods engine No 30824 at Eastleigh 9 May 1964. Although these were intended for fast goods trains they were faster than some earlier 4-6-0s and were used on holiday extras
P M ALEXANDER

Below: Urie N15 No 30736 *Excalibur* leaving Southampton on the Bournemouth-Newcastle through train. It is fitted with Lamaitre multi-jet blast pipe
P M ALEXANDER

The largest of the four groups, the London, Midland and Scottish, had the most troubled time of all before their locomotive policy was settled. Their first CME was George Hughes of the L&Y who intended to build a four-cylinder Pacific for the LNWR and West Coast main line services. The operating department, however, was dominated by Midland men who favoured a frequent service of light trains each hauled by a Midland type 4-4-0 compound. The Pacific was abandoned but Hughes built a number of his own L&Y superheated 4-6-0s to reinforce the Claughtons on the main line. These were better engines than the original saturated L&Y engines but they were clearly no permanent answer to

the problem. By 1926 it was obvious that neither East Coast competition nor the emergency of a national coal strike could be met by 4-4-0s, and Sir Henry Fowler of the Midland, who had succeeded Hughes, proposed to build a four-cylinder compound Pacific on the lines of those doing excellent work in France.

The Midland-dominated operating department conceded the fact that a more powerful locomotive was now needed but they were daunted by the size and complication of the proposed Fowler compound Pacific. They pointed to the GWR Castle, which was basking in the afterglow of its triumph on LNER metals, as the size of engine they wanted.

Left: Urie N15 No 30751 *Etarre*, fitted with Maunsell chimney, on a Southampton-Bournemouth stopping train in 1951
P M ALEXANDER

Below: Lord Nelson class No 852 *Sir Walter Raleigh* on a down *Continental Boat Express*. This engine has the small tender
JOHN ADAMS

Bottom: Lord Nelson class No 30851 *Sir Francis Drake* with Bulleid modifications leaving Southampton on the 11.30 Waterloo-Bournemouth in 1951
P M ALEXANDER

Above : Caledonian Railway 4-6-0 No 49, the first of a class of only two designed by McIntosh and built in 1903. Both engines were withdrawn in 1933

A WOOD COLLECTION

Below: The first class of 4-6-0 in Britain was the Highland Railway Jones Goods. Preserved No 103 stands on the turntable at Inverness

JOHN ADAMS

A Knight series postcard showing one of the Highland Railway Castle class 4-6-0s built in 1900
A WOOD COLLECTION

THE HIGHLAND MAIL (1,484 Feet Above Sea–Level).

The Knight Series, No 987

Glasgow and South Western Railway Manson 4-6-0 No 385 of 1903, from a Raphael Tuck 'Oilette' postcard
A WOOD COLLECTION

CORRIDOR EXPRESS (G&SWR)

Corridor Express, Caledonian Railway, leaving Stirling.

F Moore painting of one of the big Caledonian 4-6-0s of 1906 passing a North British 4-4-0 outside Stirling
A WOOD COLLECTION

F Moore view of a Hughes
4-6-0 of the Lancashire and
Yorkshire Railway near
Walkden with a Newcastle–
Liverpool train composed of
North Eastern Railway
corridor stock
A WOOD COLLECTION

A Holden 1500 class 4-6-0 of
the Great Eastern Railway
in original condition, from an
LPC card
A WOOD COLLECTION

Raphael Tuck 'Oilette'
postcard showing an LSWR
Drummond class T14 4-6-0 at
speed on the Bournemouth
main line
A WOOD COLLECTION

Above: Ex-LNWR Prince of Wales class as LMS No 25725 on a train bound for Crewe, standing in Shrewsbury station in 1938
COLOURVIEWS PICTURE LIBRARY

Below: Ex-GER B12 class No 1543 in LNER livery at Kittybrewster
CCQ

J G Robinson's stylish class 1 4-6-0 No 423 *Sir Sam Fay* for the Great Central Railway, from an LPC card
A WOOD COLLECTION

An ex-LNWR Claughton in early LMS livery, from a Raphael Tuck 'Oilette' card
A WOOD COLLECTION

F Moore painting of North Eastern Railway experiment of 1913: Sir Vincent Raven's mixed-traffic 4-6-0 No 825 with Strumph Uniflow cylinders
A WOOD COLLECTION

Above: Preserved GWR No 4079 *Pendennis Castle*
JOHN ADAMS

Below: Ex-GWR Hall class 4-6-0 No 4993 *Dalton Hall* at Bristol Temple Meads in 1961
P M ALEXANDER

Above: Light GWR 4-6-0 No 7808 *Cookham Manor*, **as seen at Shildon in 1975**
A J LAMBERT

Below: Modified Hall No 6960 *Raveningham Hall* **at the 150th Anniversary of Railways celebrations at Shildon in August 1975**
COLIN WHITE

Ex LMS Black Five
4-6-0 No 44767 with a Carlisle
to Carnforth goods on Shap
Summit in August 1967
JOHN M BOYES

LMS Royal Scot class
No 6144 *Honourable Artillery
Company* with an up London
Express leaving Chester. From
an original oil painting by
J W Petrie

King George V, GWR
**No 6000, now preserved at
Hereford** JOHN ADAMS

LMS No 5593
Kolhapur alongside WR No 7029
Clun Castle at Tyseley
P B WHITEHOUSE

Above: Ex-LSWR class S15 4-6-0 No 30843 at Basingstoke in September 1963
J B SNELL

Below: S15 No 841, as restored to Southern livery and named *Greene King*
G D KING

**Ex LNER B1 class
No 1306** *Mayflower* **at
Carnforth in 1975**   A J LAMBERT

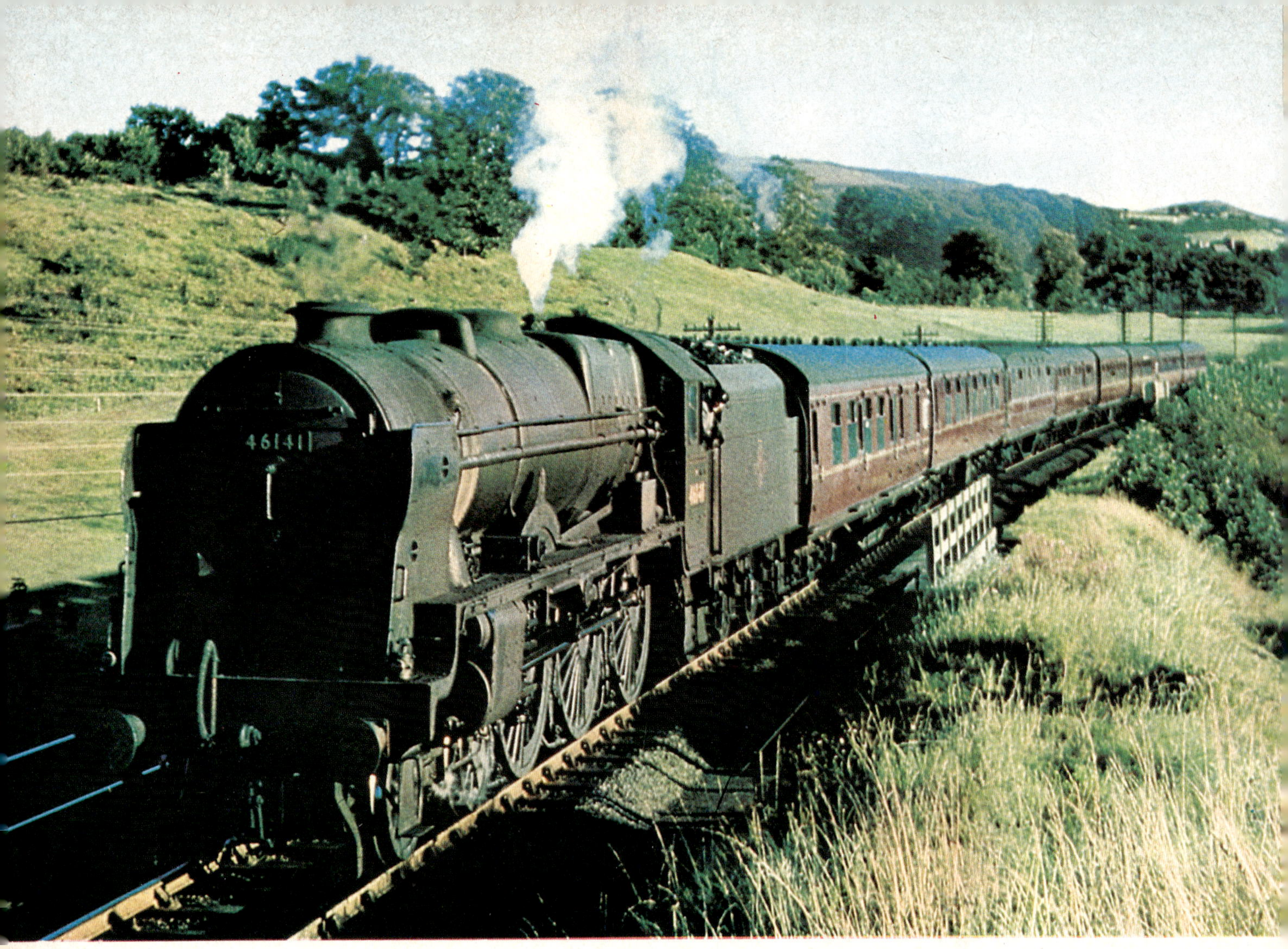
46141

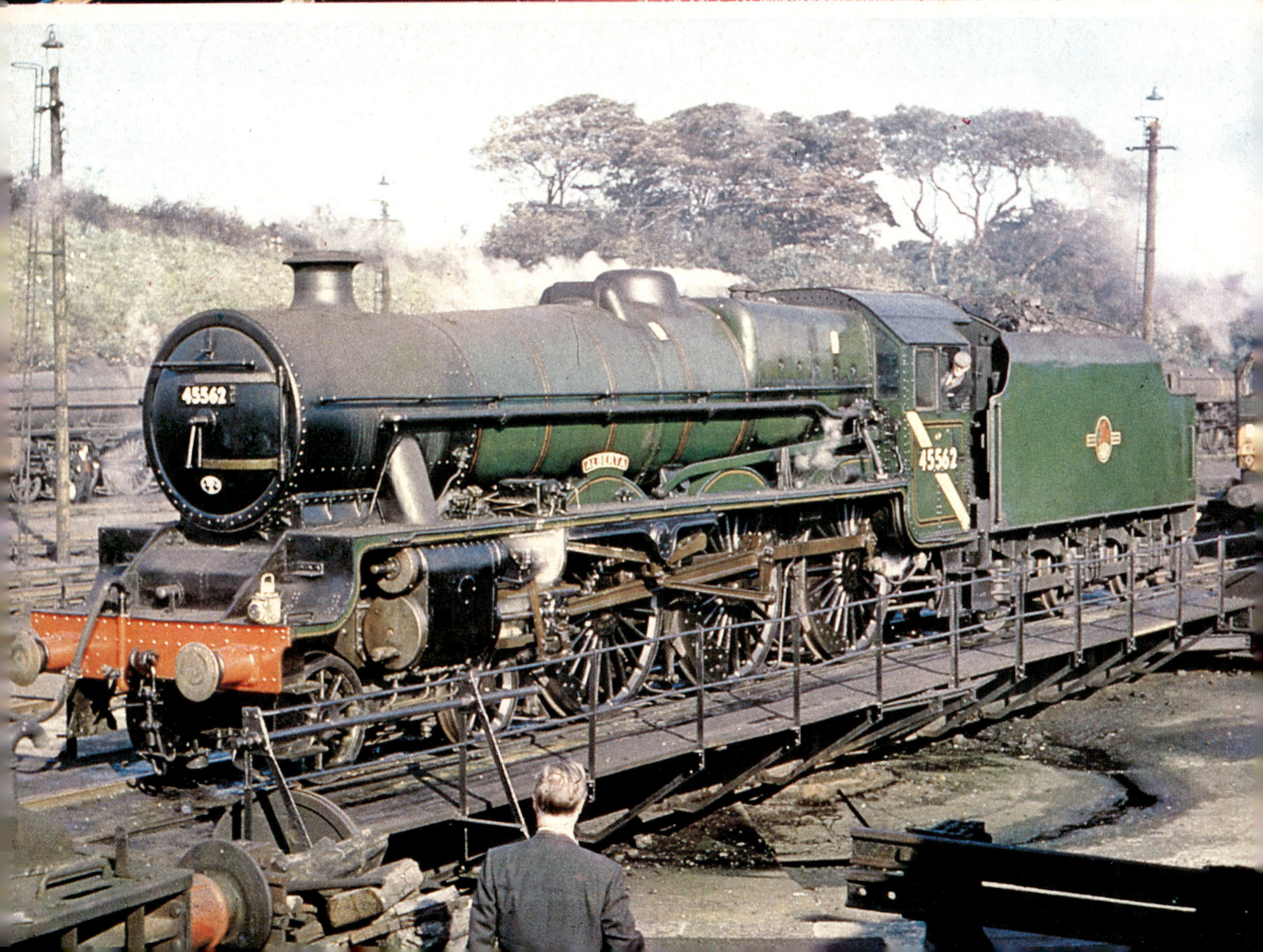
45562
45562

Towards the end of 1926 and early in 1927 No 5000 *Launceston Castle* ran trials on the LNWR main line where its superiority over the best the LMS could provide led to a decision to build a class of LMS 4-6-0s of similar size and capacity. For greater simplicity three cylinders instead of four were specified and, as time was short, the design work was shared between Derby and the North British Locomotive Company in Glasgow who were to build fifty of the engines straight from the drawing-board. Meanwhile, the prestige trains of the LMS were double headed every day.

While the new LMS 4-6-0 was taking shape, progress at Swindon forged ahead. Good as were the Castles, they were still not quite the engines which C B Collett wanted. Weight restrictions had limited their size, but by 1927 some vital bridges had been strengthened and a larger locomotive was possible. In June 1927 there emerged No 6000 *King George V*, a locomotive of truly noble proportions. The King design represented the 4-6-0 expanded almost to the maximum size possible within our restricted loading gauge; yet it retained all the grace of the earlier Churchward 4-6-0s. It was a locomotive of true Swindon ancestry, the logical enlargement of the Star and the Castle. The GWR made the most of the

Above left: Rebuilt Royal Scot No 46141
The North Staffordshire Regiment **in its final BR form, approaching Chester with a Holyhead–Euston express in the late 1950s**
COLOURVIEWS PICTURE LIBRARY

Left: Stanier Jubilee 4-6-0 No 45562 *Alberta* **at Carnforth in 1967, shortly before its withdrawal**
A J LAMBERT

Above: N1X class 4-6-0 No 32328 *Hackworth* **rebuilt from an LBSCR 4-6-4T in 1936 on a Basingstoke–Waterloo semi-fast, 15 September 1951**
P M ALEXANDER

Right: WR King No 6018 *King Henry VI* **enters Grantham station on an up Leeds express on 21 May 1948 during the BR exchange trials**
J F CLAY

occasion and posters showing 'Britain's Mightiest Passenger Locomotive' appeared all over the GWR, and cheap excursions, hauled by King class locomotives, conveyed hundreds of visitors to the Swindon works. The 'mightiest' claim was based on a nominal tractive effort which topped the 40,000 lb mark. The engine most likely to challenge such a claim was the new LNER A3 class Pacific, which had its valve gear modified as a result of the 1925 exchanges and a 220 lb boiler. LNER expresses were very heavy but, in 1927, were easily timed as compared with the best GWR bookings. It was not until 1935 that the everyday work of the Kings was challenged.

An engine less spectacular than the King, but which was perhaps destined ultimately to be more important, was first introduced when a Saint class engine No 2925 *Saint Martin* was rebuilt with 6 ft driving wheels instead of 6 ft 8 in. This formed the prototype of a mixed-traffic class faster than the 2-6-0s. In 1928, many more of these engines named after 'Halls' were built and they were destined to reach a class total of 330 machines.

In the late summer of 1927 the new LMS Royal Scot 4-6-0s began to be delivered from Glasgow and in the autumn *The Royal Scot* express started to run non-stop to Carlisle. The Royal Scots had some growing pains but their appearance was a tonic to the LMS, where morale had fallen during the troubled early years. They responded well when the LMS accelerated their main line services from 1932 onwards. In September 1933 the LMS ran a number of specials to Coventry and back carrying guests of a motor car company. Some very fast running was made over the gently undulating LNWR main line and, in the course of two days, the Royal Scot class engine No 6129 *Comet* travelled 235 miles, with an average load of 273 tons, at an average speed of 79.6 mph.

On the LNER Gresley retained his faith in the Pacific for the heaviest trains. However, there were parts of the LNER which needed new motive power but which could not accept large and heavy engines. These needs were, at first, met by modifications to existing designs. Lentz poppet valves were tried on some former GER 4-6-0s and Caprotti valves on some four-cylinder GCR engines, and later feed water heaters were added to GER 4-6-0s. A new design of three-cylinder 4-6-0s of the B17 or Sandringham class were built for the GER main line in 1928. These were built to very strict weight restrictions and much of the design work was done by the North British Locomotive Company. Later they were used on the GCR main line where they proved to be very fast but acquired a reputation for rough riding. An extensive rebuilding of the GER 4-6-0s began in 1932. They were given larger boilers and a modern front end and these modifications brought the class up to a standard of performance comparable with the Sandringhams. Some of the North Eastern three-cylinder mixed-traffic 4-6-0s were rebuilt by Gresley with his 2 and 1 valve gear and front end design. This resulted in a freer running engine with a lower coal consumption. The LNER did very well during the depression of the 1930s by keeping traffic moving with the minimum of capital expenditure.

The LMS were not convinced that it was good policy to modernise old locomotives and they usually replaced rather than rebuilt, but an exception was made with the former

Above left: No 6026 *King John*
hurries downhill near Patney
with the down *Cornish Riviera*
after a snow shower
P M ALEXANDER

Above: No 6016 *King Edward V*
leaving Dainton Tunnel with the
8.30 Plymouth-Paddington on
13 September 1950
P M ALEXANDER

Left: No 6013 *King Henry VIII*
running in on a Bath to Swindon
stopping train
P M ALEXANDER

Above: No 4951 *Pendeford Hall*
on a stock train. Although
photographed in BR days this
engine retains its small
low-sided tender
P M ALEXANDER

Left: GWR King class 4-6-0
No 6009 *King Charles II*
arriving at Torquay with the
down *Torbay Express* **in August**
1934
J F CLAY

LNWR Claughtons. A serious attempt was made to rejuvenate these engines to provide better running mates for the Royal Scots. In 1928 a number of Claughtons were given larger boilers and some were fitted with Caprotti valves but in 1930 a more extensive 'rebuilding' took place which was really more of a 'replacement'. The enlarged Claughton boiler was mated with the three cylinders of a Royal Scot to produce a slightly smaller engine that was nicknamed the 'Baby Scot'. The LMS authorities considered that this name lacked dignity and when the war memorial Claughton *Patriot* was replaced by a 'Baby Scot' the class name of was officially encouraged and in course of time the official view prevailed.

In 1932 the post of Chief Mechanical Engineer of the LMS went to a former GWR man W A (later Sir William) Stanier. The new chief embarked on a policy of replacement which has aptly been called 'a mighty restocking'. Under Stanier, Pacific-type locomotives were built for the heaviest trains but there was no disposition to go as far as Gresley or later Bulleid in adopting 'The Big Engine Policy'. Stanier aimed at building just enough Pacifics for the cream of the traffic and meet other needs with 4-6-0s. To this end he built hundreds of 4-6-0s. The first new type was an adaptation of the Patriot class with a taper boiler based on GWR practice. It was thought that this blending of design features that were well proved in practice could hardly fail, but the Stanier three-cylinder 4-6-0s, known later as the 'Jubilees' were at first as uncertain in everyday performance as the Claughtons ever had been. By 1937, however, the re-draughting of the boiler, and more superheating surface, raised the class to a much higher standard of everyday performance.

The second design of Stanier 4-6-0 achieved a success that most probably exceeded the hopes of its designer. This was a two-cylinder mixed-traffic engine, of much the same size as a GWR Hall, later to be generally known as the 'Black Five'. The class was meant to take over the duties of the LNWR Princes and a number of other older 4-6-0s of similar size. It was soon found that, with a modern front end, six-feet driving wheels were no handicap to speeds up to, and at times slightly over, 90 mph. These so called 'mixed-traffic' engines were also first-class medium-sized express engines destined ultimately to reach a class total of 842 machines.

Below: No 4930 *Hagley Hall* **approaching Box Tunnel on the 11.23 Bath to Swindon in October 1952**
P M ALEXANDER

Right: No 7801 *Anthony Manor* climbs towards Talerddig Summit with a freight train
P M ALEXANDER

Far right: No 6829 *Burminster Grange* coasts down Dainton Bank with the 8.45 am Plymouth to Manchester and Liverpool in March 1950
P M ALEXANDER

Below: No 10440 of the Hughes 4-cylinder 4-6-0 class built in 1923 with superheater and piston valves

L M S   10440

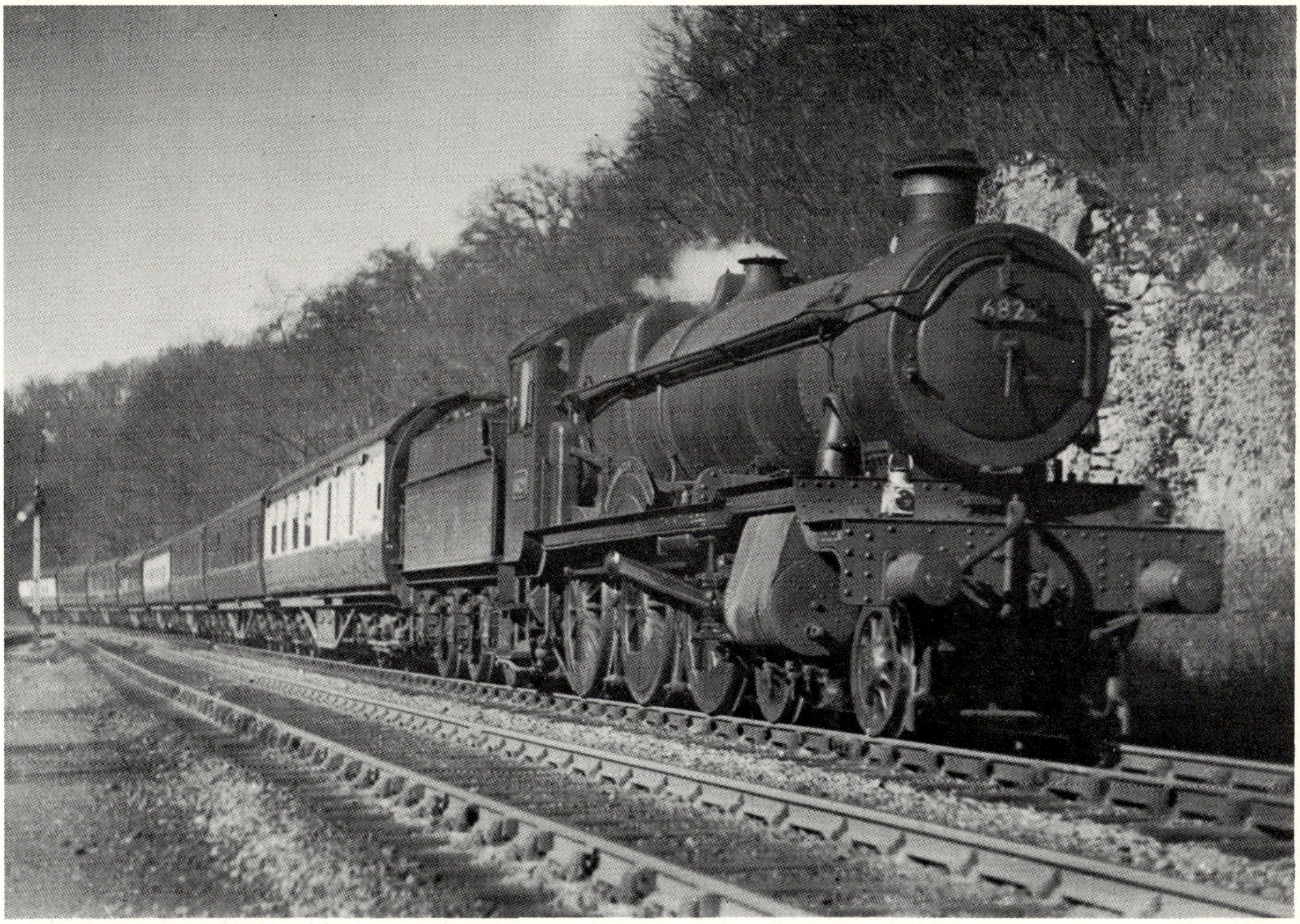

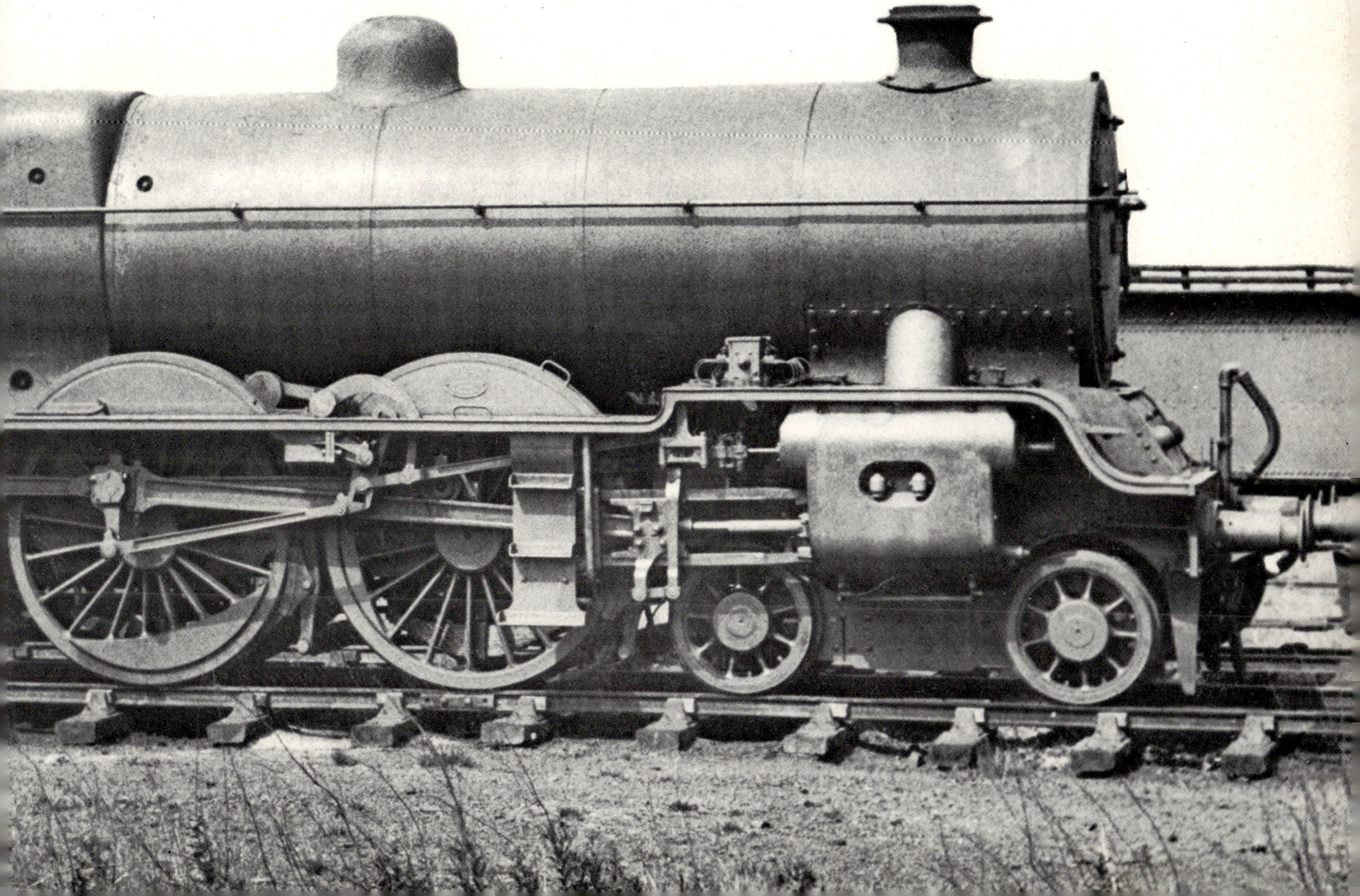

Top right: Royal Scot class 4-6-0 No 6115 new and un-named soon after delivery from the Queen's Park Works of the North British Locomotive Co in September 1927
A W FLOWERS

Centre right: Royal Scots gave trouble with drifting steam and smoke. No 6109 *Royal Engineer* is shown with an early arrangement of small plates and a conical smokebox door
P M ALEXANDER

Below: No 6148 *The Manchester Regiment* hauling a main line express near Lichfield in June 1931

The 1930s had seen a general advance in locomotive efficiency and the GWR, who had led British practice for a quarter of a century found they had some formidable rivals. Swindon, however, went quietly on its way building engines well suited to the GWR traffic demands. C B Collett was satisfied with thirty Kings for the heaviest traffic and he added to the number of Castles. Some very exciting high-speed running was made by Castle class engines. On 6 June 1932 No 5006 *Tregenna Castle* brought the 195-ton *Cheltenham Flyer* up the 77.3 miles from Swindon to Paddington in 56 min 47 sec start to stop – 39 miles had been run at an average speed of 90 mph. The tendency of the road was gently downhill but the GWR authorities were anxious to prove that gravity alone was not responsible, so they took the recorders back to Swindon in a 210-ton train hauled by No 5005 *Manorbier Castle* in 60 min 01 sec. As if this was not enough they then stopped an up Bristol express at Swindon and rushed the recorders back to Paddington at

Below: No 10469 built by the LMS makes a fine show while picking up water at the head of a West Coast express

speeds less sensational but still very fast. Within three and a half hours three different Castles had covered 220 miles at an average speed of 80 mph. In June 1937 No 5039 *Rhuddlan Castle* with 235 tons covered 50 miles at an average of 90 mph.

The GWR mixed-traffic stock was augmented by more Halls, and a number of 2-6-0 engines were replaced either by the 'Grange' class 4-6-0, which was in all essentials a Hall with 5 ft 8 in wheels, or by the smaller 'Manor' class which could work on routes with more rigid weight restrictions.

When the Second World War broke out mixed-traffic engines proved to be of great value and the LMS Black Fives shared with Gresley's large 2-6-2s of the 'Green Arrow' class the honour of being called 'the engines which won the war'. In 1941 Sir Nigel Gresley died and was succeeded on the LNER by Edward Thompson who wanted to put into effect a restocking policy similar to that of Stanier on the LMS. He built a two-cylinder mixed-traffic 4-6-0 which was, in effect, an LNER version of the Hall and the Black Five. The first was named *Springbok* but the class was more usually known by its numerical classification as 'B1'. The B1s were destined to be as useful to the LNER as the Black Fives had been to the LMS and they reached a class total of 410 engines. Thompson's rebuilding of some three-cylinder Sandringham class engines with two cylinders was less successful. He rebuilt more of the NER three-cylinder mixed-traffic engines with a modern front end but with three sets of Walschaert's gear, instead of two, and the Gresley derived motion.

On the GWR C B Collett retired in 1941 and was replaced by F W Hawksworth, who continued in the Churchward tradition but made some significant changes in boiler proportions. The GWR practice of moderate superheat had proved to be less successful on the LMS, but Collett had shown no interest in Stanier's experience. Hawksworth, however, worried by reports of bad steaming with wartime coal, built some Halls with enlarged superheaters. These were known as 'Modified Halls'. Towards the end of the war, Hawksworth built a two-cylinder 4-6-0 with 6 ft 3 in

wheels designed to be a cheaper alternative to the Castle. These were named after Counties and at times ran very well, but after the war the building of Castles was resumed. The new engines had more superheating surface.

The LMS continued to build Black Fives and here, again, the later examples had more superheating surface. After the war some were built with Caprotti valve gear and one experimental engine had outside Stephenson's Link Motion. The most exciting 4-6-0 development during the war years was the rebuilding of the Royal Scots. There had been an ill-fated experiment with a 900 lb Schmidt-Henshall water tube boiler on a compound version of a Royal Scot named *Fury*. This had a fatal boiler explosion and ran a very small mileage. Stanier rebuilt it as a conventional Royal Scot with a taper boiler in 1936: it was named *British Legion*. In 1942 two Jubilee class engines were fitted with a shortened version of this boiler with a double chimney and, in 1943, this boiler was tried on a Royal Scot with improved valves and steam passages. The rebuilding was a great success and in the converted Royal Scot the GWR King met its most formidable rival for the title of Britain's most powerful 4-6-0. More Royal Scots were rebuilt, and when they passed into national ownership on 1 January 1948 over half the class had been

rebuilt. The rebuilding was extended to the Patriot class and all the remaining Royal Scots were converted in a few years. The LMS had a most potent second line of powerful 4-6-0s to reinforce their Pacifics. The most serious criticism of these efficient locomotives was their tendency to develop rough riding with increased mileage.

The nationalised era of British Railways dawned with the Pacific well entrenched as the premier express type on three of the four groups, but with the 4-6-0 still the most numerous type. The Great Western alone remained faithful to the 4-6-0 for its heaviest trains – an ironical position for the line which had built Britain's first Pacific.

Left: Royal Scot class No 46158, still unrebuilt in BR days but with high-sided tender and smoke-deflector plates, heads an up express near Brinklow in October 1950
C F OLDHAM

Below: Rebuilt Claughton No 6017 *Breadalbane* on Bushey water troughs with an up express in June 1933

Left: Jubilee No 45602 *British Honduras* passing Mangotsfield on the 13.17 Sunday train from Bristol to York
P M ALEXANDER

Right: No 5954 of the Patriot class which replaced some of the Claughtons. Some parts of the original engines were used in the first rebuilds but later engines were all new
R G JARVIS

Below: Stanier 3-cylinder Jubilee class engine No 5662 in original condition with low superheat domeless boiler
R G JARVIS

Right: No 45616 *Malta GC* passing Crawford on an Edinburgh-Euston express. This engine has the small Midland-type tender
ERIC TREACY

Far right: Stanier Black Five mixed-traffic engine No 5058 in original condition at Nottingham Midland in 1935
T G HEPBURN

Below: Caprotti valve-geared Class 5 No 44746 at work
P M ALEXANDER

Below right: Class 5 No 44841 passing Newton Harcourt with an up excursion train on 28 October 1950
P M ALEXANDER

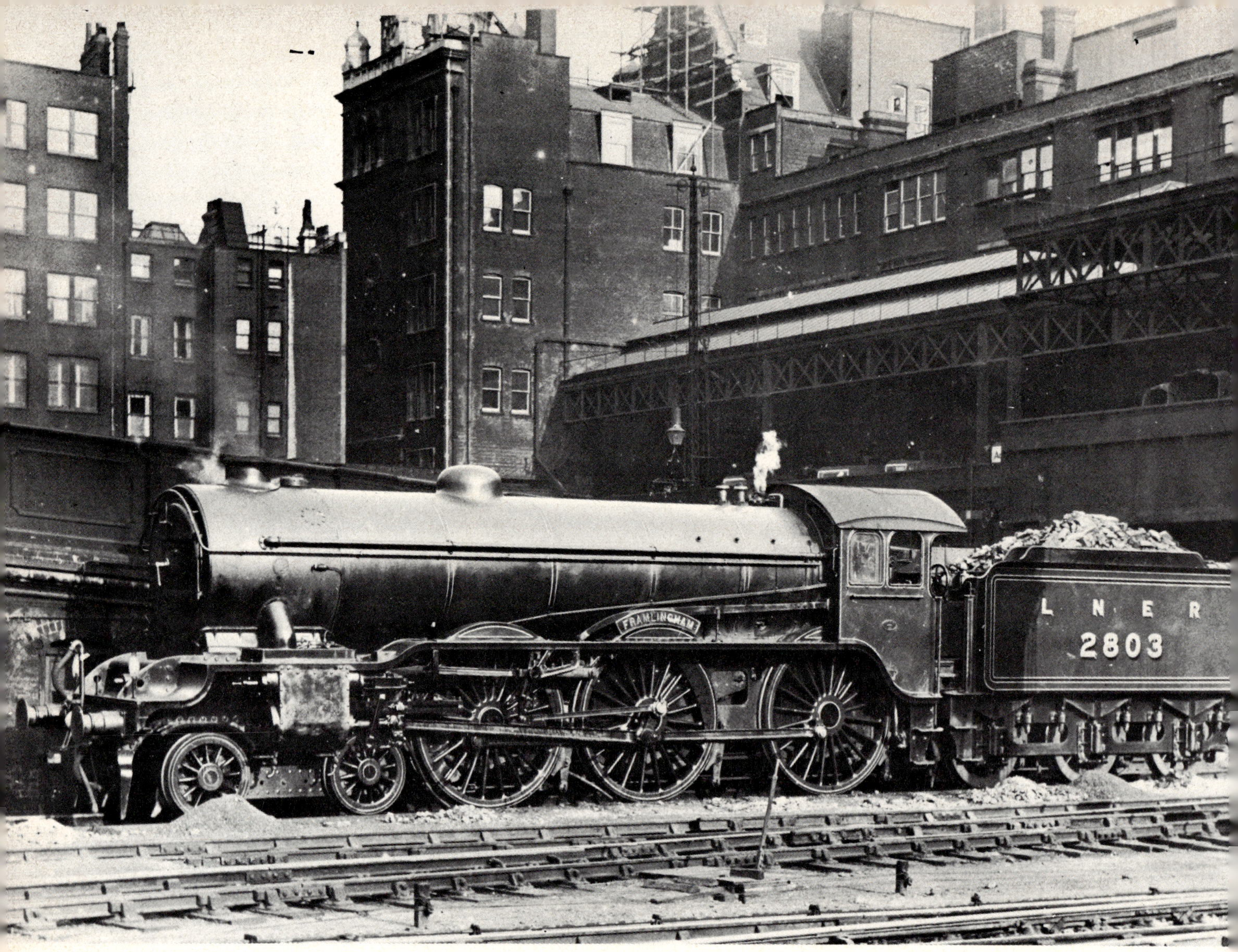
FRAMLINGHAM
L N E R
2803

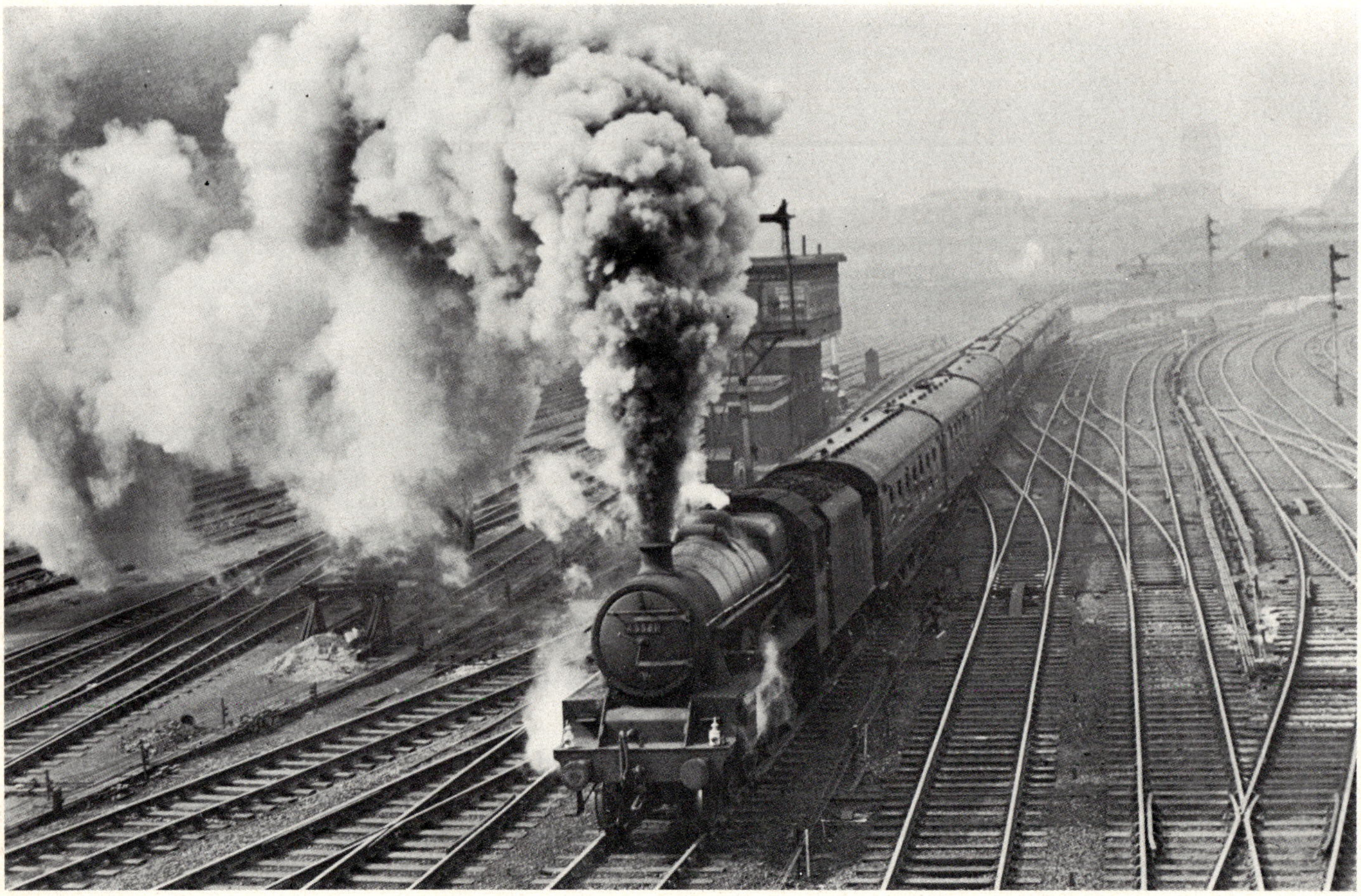

Above left: LNER Class B17 No 2803 *Framlingham* at Liverpool Street shortly after construction. This engine has the small GER - type tender

Below left: No 45581 *Bihar and Orissa* leaving Edge Hill on a Liverpool-Hull express
ERIC TREACY

Above: No 45465 at Crieff on a two-coach Gleneagles branch train
M POPE

Below: No 5443 of the GCR Glanalmond class mixed-traffic engines photographed at Neasden
JOHN ADAMS

Above left: B17 No 61672 *West Ham United* **passing Bury St Edmunds Junction in early BR days**

Above right: Rebuilt B12/3 class No 61564 climbing Ledham Bank with a Felixstowe-Liverpool Street train.
P M ALEXANDER

Below: No 61417 as rebuilt by Edward Thompson with three sets of Walschaert's gear leaving the King Edward Bridge, Newcastle, with a fast freight
ERIC TREACY

Below right: The first County class 4-6-0, No 1000 *County of Middlesex*, **with double chimney, passing Thingley Junction with the 17.05 Paddington-Plymouth via Bristol**
P M ALEXANDER

4-6-0s Under Nationalisation

THE world was bleak enough for the railway industry after the First World War, but after the Second War the situation was indescribably worse. Some drastic commercial restructuring was clearly inevitable, but few locomotive enthusiasts, whatever their political persuasion, welcomed nationalisation from 1 January 1948. They feared that dull uniformity would replace the variety of designs which had made the study of the steam locomotive so interesting. At first, however, their worst fears were not realised and one of the first things to happen was something enthusiasts had been longing for – a full scale interchange of locomotives. These trials were officially declared to be for the purpose of providing preliminary data for the designing of a standard range of locomotives combining the good points of all engines of the pre-grouping era.

The value of the 1948 exchange trials was lessened by the number of speed restrictions imposed because track had not fully recovered from wartime neglect. In the heavy express class the lowest coal consumptions per dbhp were registered by the ER A4 and the LMR Duchess class Pacifics but some of the most sparkling running, and certainly the highest dbhps per ton of engine weight, were to the credit of the converted Royal Scot. The GWR King was not allowed on the LMR or SR main lines because of tight clearances and it achieved nothing of any note on the ER. A brighter chapter in the story of the King class was, however, destined to follow. In the mixed-traffic class the Class 5 4-6-0s from the WR, the ER and the LMR were pitted against the larger SR West Country class Pacific and this engine, driven hard with a willing fireman, out-classed the power outputs of the 4-6-0s.

In the post-war world locomotive coal was of a more variable quality than in pre-war days and engines were expected to run greater mileages with less attention. Under these conditions the designers of the nationalised concern decided that the wide firebox of Pacific-type locomotives was an advantage. Everyone had been impressed by the excellent uphill performance of the SR West Country class engine on the Highland but this was the result of skilled driving and very arduous firing. Later, it was realised that such performance could not be expected every day and that slipping could limit the value of any Pacific on such grades. This was proved later when West Country class engines were used on the heavily graded Somerset and Dorset main line. They ran some very promising individual trips but their everyday performance was so affected by slipping that their maximum loads were fixed at a figure no higher than that for the Class 5 4-6-0s. Few, if any, 4-6-0s could, however, have matched the high drawbar hps developed by the West Country Pacifics at high speeds on level or moderately graded routes.

The Class 6 standard Pacifics of the Clan class were disappointing and the original intention to use them in regular service over the Highland main line was never carried out. Some shrewd observers believe that they would have been better built as 4-6-0s or 4-8-0s. The idea of building a Class 5 Pacific was abandoned and a Class 5 4-6-0, using a boiler similar to that of the LMR Black Five, was substituted. This was known as the '73' class and some later examples had Caprotti valves. For service over lines with very rigid load restrictions a slightly smaller Class 4 4-6-0, known as the '75' class, was introduced. This class undertook duties

similar to those given to the GWR Manors on lines such as the Cambrian.

While the 1948 exchanges were taking place the Rugby Testing Station, due to be opened on 19 October 1948, was approaching completion. The Swindon test plant was also brought up to modern standards and during the 1950s locomotive testing was conducted on a much more scientific basis. Running at constant speed on the plant, or on controlled road tests, produced results of much greater significance than the old-style variable speed dynamometer car tests.

One of the greatest problems facing the people who operated the railways in the 1950s was the very variable quality of steam locomotive performance. The steam locomotive had always been subjective in performance, as it depended so much on the skill and hard work of the footplate crew and on the standard of preparation. In the 1950s it became increasingly difficult to get skilled workers while the rigours of work on the footplate, or in the running sheds, compared so unattractively with more highly-paid employment at regular hours in warm and dry factories. With poor coal and long mileages, it is little wonder that the reputation for reliability, even of famous classes of engines with immaculate records before the war, began to suffer. The 4-6-0s suffered with the rest, but 4-6-2 and 2-6-2 engines were by no means free from steaming troubles which affected wide and narrow fireboxes alike. The best results were obtained from those locomotives which had sophisticated blast pipe and chimney arrangements, and research on the test plants was directed towards improved draughting designed to make locomotives more adaptable to low-grade fuels.

As a result of scientific investigation it was found possible to improve the steaming rates of some locomotives considerably by making simple, cheap adjustments to the existing single blast pipe and chimney proportions. The GWR Manor class was an example; so was the wide-fireboxed ER 2-6-2 of the V2 class. GWR enthusiasts had been dismayed by the results of the 1948 exchanges when their King and Hall class engines failed to repeat the triumphs of the Castles in 1925/27. Although the occasional good run still took place on the WR, there was little indication from everyday performance that unaltered WR locomotives would ever regain their pre-war standards. Some patient work had, however, been going on behind the scenes at Swindon and, in the summer of 1953, the results were shown in dramatic fashion by the publication of a photograph showing No 6001 *King Edward VII* running at a steady 60 mph on a slight up grade with a vast train of 25 coaches weighing around 800 tons.

The Kings, improved by more superheating surface and various re-draughting modifications, had produced a loco-

Left: No 1018 *County of Leicester* between St Austell and Par with the 11.25 Sunday train from Penzance to Wolverhampton
P M ALEXANDER

Above right: No 1020 *County of Monmouth* with single chimney at Cardiff Canton shed on 10 September 1950
P M ALEXANDER

Right: No 7813 *Freshford Manor* and No 1018 *County of Leicester* climbing Hemerdon bank with a stopping train
P M ALEXANDER

motive capable of a higher steaming rate which could use lower-grade coal with greater confidence. As a result of these improvements the WR was able to re-introduce the *Bristolian* express on its pre-war booking of 105 min for the 118½ miles from Paddington to Bristol. During the first week No 6015 *King Richard III* showed its ability by cutting ten minutes from this fast booking. As in pre-war days it was soon found that Castles were quite able to keep up the timing.

One of the reasons for the excellent performance of the converted Royal Scot in the 1948 exchanges had been the double blast pipe and chimney, and following test-running by a Duchess class LMR Pacific on the WR in 1955, a double chimney was fitted to No 6015 *King Richard III*. The double-chimneyed King proved to be more free running in the higher speed ranges and in course of time the entire class was altered to conform. There were further plans to use Caprotti valves and roller bearings in a more drastic re-building of the Kings but this was carried no further when diesel traction replaced steam on the WR. The double-chimneyed King, pressed closely by the converted Royal Scots, represented the British 4-6-0 in its final stage of development.

Double chimneys were fitted to some of the Castle class 4-6-0s and to the County class. The first of the Counties had been built with a double chimney but, because it was in-correctly proportioned and gave disappointing results, the remainder of the class had single chimneys. Later research suggested a better form of double chimney which unfor-tunately rather spoilt the look of the engine. The double-chimneyed Castles were better in the higher-speed ranges than those with single chimneys, but the difference was less than had been the case with the Kings.

The end of steam traction on British Railways was fore-shadowed by the publication of the modernisation plan in 1955. It is sad that some re-draughting modifications came too late to have much effect. The Stanier Jubilee class 4-6-0s, for example, had started badly but were improved by enlarged superheaters and re-draughting so that from 1937 onwards they were running very well. Then the rigours of wartime operation caused another decline in average standards. In the post-war world the Jubilees occasionally ran as well as ever they had done but the average standard was variable. One was tested at Rugby and re-draughting alterations were suggested, but by then time was running out for steam and only a few of the class were altered before the large-scale building of diesels drove the remaining steam engines to the scrap-heap.

No 46164 *The Artists Rifleman* **leaving Euston with the down** *Merseyside Express* **on 16 June 1954**
ERIC TREACY

Left: No **46142** *The York and Lancaster Regiment* **approaching Chester on a Holyhead-Euston express in August 1951**
P M ALEXANDER

Top: Converted Royal Scot No 46155 *The Lancer* **at Crewe North shed in 1952**
J F CLAY

Above: Rebuilt Patriot No 45536 *Private W Wood VC* **climbing Llanvihangel Bank with a Plymouth-Manchester through train, in September 1952**
P M ALEXANDER

Left: No 46157 *The Royal Artilleryman* **near Wigston North Junction on an up Manchester-St Pancras express in 1958**
J F CLAY

Right: Thompson class B1 mixed-traffic engine passing Santon Downham near Thetford with a Norwich-Cambridge train on 25 May 1951
P M ALEXANDER

Below: No 46150 *The Life Guardsman* **leaving Chester on the down** *Irish Mail* **on 20 August 1951**
P M ALEXANDER

If we are to offer a proper evaluation of the British 4-6-0s we must consider the timings put up by these splendid locomotives, but to do so adequately would require a separate book at least as large as this one. It is possible, therefore, only to tell of a few of the highlights, and some of the events of the final two decades take an honourable place. During the 1920s the British 4-6-0 reached the zenith of its reputation when Castles visited LNER and LMS metals in interchange trials with such resounding success that three of the four groups chose 4-6-0s instead of Pacifics for their heaviest passenger duties. It seemed in 1927 that the 4-6-0 victory was complete. The very success of the GWR engines had, however, inspired others to adopt their essential features of valve and front end design. From 1935 onwards, additional refinements, based on the work of A Chapelon in France, were added to Pacific locomotives. As every sportsman knows a good 'big-un' will beat a good 'little-un', and so it was that in the years 1935 to 1939 most of the British records of power and speed passed from 4-6-0s to 4-6-2s.

The 4-6-0 did not relinquish its pre-eminence easily and the best 4-6-0 performances should not be underestimated. To the very end 4-6-0s pressed their larger rivals hard. The largest British 4-6-0s were the GWR Kings and these were placed in power class 8 along with the largest Pacifics. A sustained ihp of 2,300 on the plant was claimed for a double-chimneyed King and, although this was less than the 2,900

sustained under similar circumstances by the larger LMR Duchess class Pacific, it was still well above anything required under normal operating conditions. What a continuous ihp of just over 2,000 meant in haulage capacity was shown when the single-chimney King No 6001 *King Edward VII* hauled a 25-coach load of 798 tons from near Reading to Stoke Gifford Junction and back at the normal speeds of a South Wales express. This of course did not mean that ordinary expresses could be allowed to load up to twenty-five bogies, as special test conditions with two firemen could not be provided for everyday running. The aim of post-war operating was to make the everyday job well within the capacity of the loco-motive. Loads were related to the most economical output of the engine rather than to its test house maximum. The result of scientific rostering was that the everyday loading of GWR expresses in the 1950s was normally less than during the 1930s.

The heaviest loads hauled by 4-6-0 locomotives in post-war Britain were to be found on the former LNWR section of the LMR behind Class 7 converted Royal Scots or rebuilt Patriots. The 15-coach train was commonplace and sixteen or seventeen bogies behind one 4-6-0 were not unknown. A converted Royal Scot brought a 515-ton train up from Stafford to Euston in 122 min net time for 133½ miles, while a rebuilt Patriot ran up from Crewe 158.1 miles to Euston in a net time of 149 min. Although classified as Class 7, these

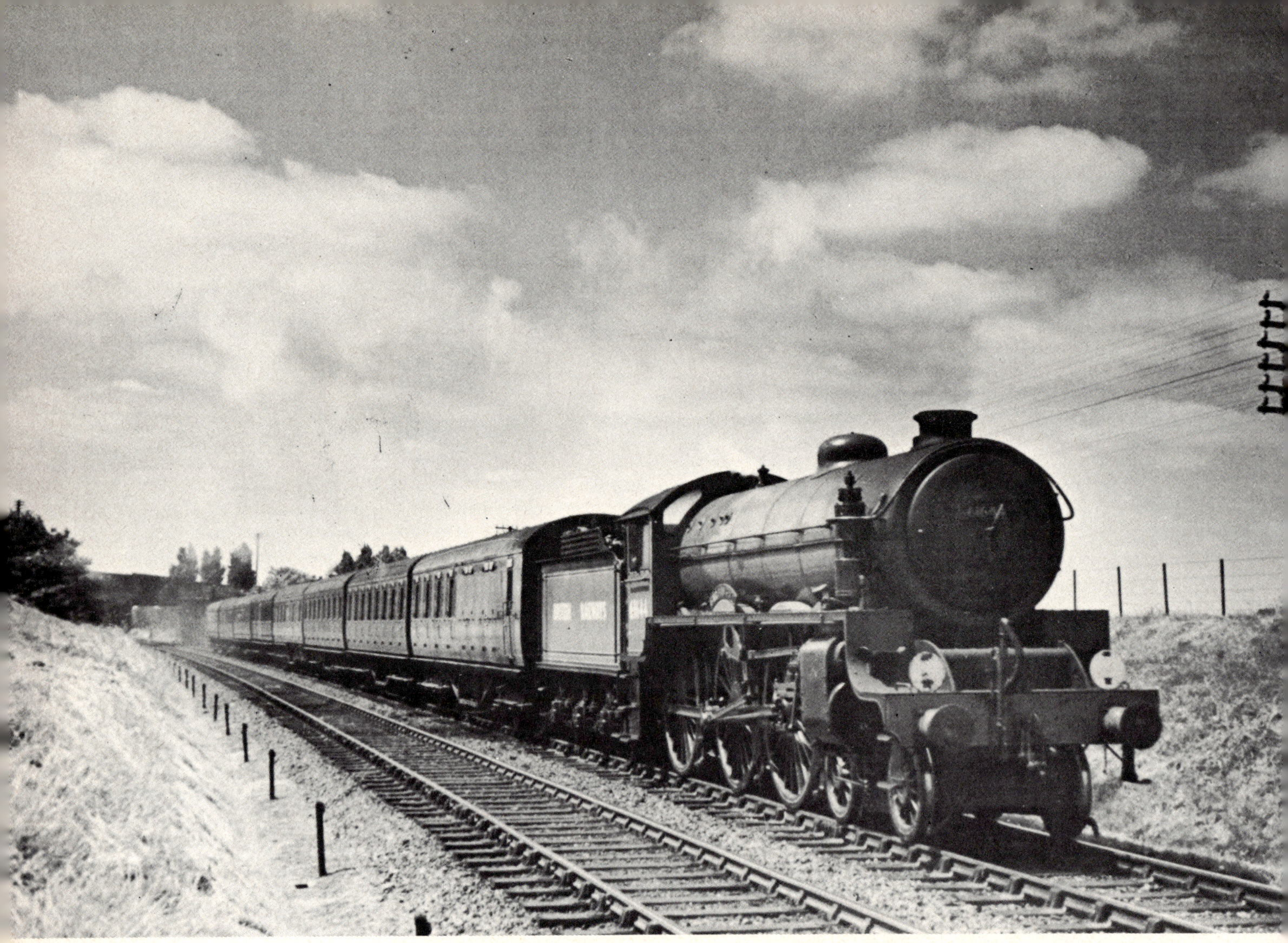

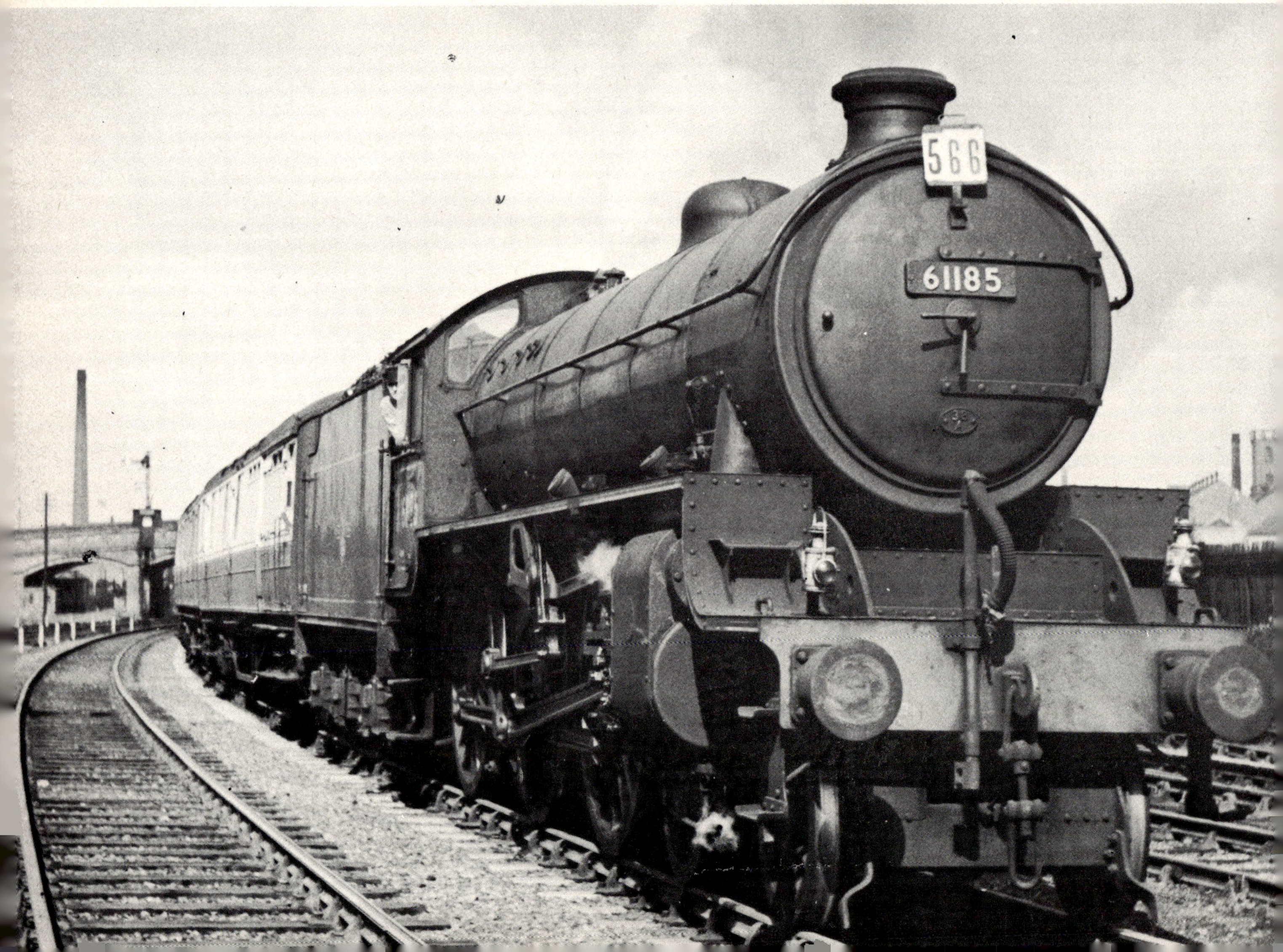
566
61185

LMR 4-6-0s came close to the Kings in drawbar hp and they almost certainly held the record among 4-6-0s for dbhp per ton of engine weight. On the test plant a Royal Scot reached over 2100 ihp on Grade 2 coal but general indications are that the greater adhesion weight and tractive effort gave the King an advantage when starting or climbing very steep gradients at low speeds. The lighter Royal Scot needed less power to move itself and in the middle-speed ranges dbhps were similar; the 1782 dbhp recorded by a Royal Scot during the 1948 exchanges was never significantly beaten by a King. In the higher ranges of speed the better riding of the King was an asset and more three figure maxima are credited to the Western engines.

The highest speed recorded by any British 4-6-0 hauling a train would appear to be approximately 107 mph near Lavington by No 6015 *King Richard III* shortly after being fitted with a double chimney. Unfortunately exaggerated accounts of this incident were circulated by over-enthusiastic partisans with the result that some doubts were raised. A careful examination of the evidence supports a maximum speed in the region of 107 mph. A number of maximum speeds in the 100-103 mph range were recorded by King and Castle class engines at various locations on the WR, and 100 mph was claimed for a converted Royal Scot between Luton and Bedford on the former Midland main line. Down-hill speeds are, however, less significant than speeds attained with no help from gravity: the double-chimneyed Kings could reach 90 mph with over 300 tons, and so could the double-chimneyed Castles with over 250 tons on dead level track.

Although these records of power and speed were surpassed by larger Pacific-type locomotives, the best of the 4-6-0s were not disgraced in a size for size comparison. In the ordinary day to day running of a railway the Class 5 mixed-traffic 4-6-0s played a most valuable role. In an emergency, such

Above left: No 61644 *Earlham Hall*, rebuilt by Thompson from class B17 to the 2-cylinder B2 class, passing Marks Tey with a Liverpool-Norwich train
P M ALEXANDER

Below left: B1 No 61185 leaving Leicester, Belgrave Road, with a Skegness excursion train
D W WEBB

Below: No 6021 *King Richard II* slips swiftly and easily down Hatton Bank and through Warwick station with the 12 noon Snow Hill-Paddington express in June 1961
J F CLAY

Left: Double-chimneyed King No 6016 *King Edward V* climbs towards Dainton Summit with steam and noise with the 9.30 Paddington-Plymouth express on 2 February 1959
D S FISH

Below: Double-chimneyed Castle No 5022 *Wigmore Castle* passing Fenny Compton with an up Birmingham-Paddington express on 13 June 1959
MICHAEL MASON

Bottom No 1022 *County of Northampton* at Swindon shed in May 1956. This unsightly type of double chimney proved to be more efficient
J F CLAY

87

locomotives could take over almost any job. The most spectacular example of the versatility of a Class 5 mixed-traffic engine was when No 7904 *Fountains Hall* took over the up *Bristolian* and ran from Little Somerford to Paddington 89.7 miles in 72 min 10 sec with a pass to pass average of 80 mph for 71.6 miles. In coal consumption, on the only valid basis of coal burnt per dbhp hr, there was little difference between the best 4-6-2 and 4-6-0 engines. The day to day difference between engines of the same class was often greater than the variation between classes. The wide-fireboxed engines certainly had an advantage on long non-stop runs, although the unconverted Royal Scot class 4-6-0 No 6113 *Cameronian* as long ago as 1928 ran non-stop from Euston to Glasgow, 401 miles, it was with a moderate load at a moderate speed. Over shorter distances and especially on trains making frequent stops and facing steep short gradients, a strong case can be made for the 4-6-0 because of its comparative freedom from slipping.

The final years of steam were years of indifference and neglect punctuated occasionally, right up to the last, by stirring individual performances often on enthusiasts' specials. On such occasions enginemen often enjoyed a glorious last fling and gave a startling vista of what steam performance might have been had there been no war and had scientific testing begun ten years earlier. The last public service train hauled by steam ran on 3 August 1968 headed by a Black Five 4-6-0. Since then preserved locomotives have occasionally been allowed a run on the main lines. Among these have been a number of once-famous 4-6-0s and their re-appearance has been the cause of great joy to travellers and photographers. May it long continue.

Top left: No 73078 and Stanier No 44976 climbing from Arrochar with a Glasgow train on 27 May 1959
S E TEASDALE

Top: Standard class 5 No 73014 approaches Droitwich Spa with a Birmingham-Gloucester stopping train
J D MILLS

Left: BR Standard class 5 No 73004 at Birmingham New Street waiting to work a Leicester semi-fast
A W FLOWERS

Above: Caprotti class 5 No 73144 on the 8.26 am Leicester-St Pancras approaching Wigston North Junction in August 1957
J F CLAY

Far left: Standard class 4
No 75005 climbs towards
Talerdigg Summit
P B WHITEHOUSE

Above: Class 4 No 75005 at
work on the Cambrian main line
P B WHITEHOUSE

Left: The preserved No 6100
Royal Scot at Bressingham
Steam Museum in June 1972
J F CLAY

Below: No 7029 *Clun Castle*
heads an enthusiasts' special
through Corby Glen on 17
September 1967
T C HEPBURN

Left: The preserved double-chimneyed Jubilee No 5596 *Bahamas* at Dinting Steam Centre in July 1974
J F CLAY

Centre left: The preserved Big Goods Highland Railway 4-6-0 No 103 at Bedford shed after being used in filming *Those Magnificent Men in Their Flying Machines* in May 1964
MERVYN MASON

Below: No 6000 *King George V* leaving Chester with an enthusiasts' special on 26 April 1975 J F CLAY

Appendix

In this appendix, it is realised, there is no clear distinction between a 'rebuilding' and a 'replacement' nor between a 'major' and a 'minor' rebuilding. It is not claimed that the demarkation lines used here are the only ones possible. Other interpretations could be given equal justification.

The designation of a locomotive as 'express passenger', 'mixed-traffic' or 'goods' is based on the intentions of the designer when the engine was first built; it is not a judgement on performance. Modern 'mixed-traffic' types, such as the Class 5s built in such large numbers by the GWR, the LMS and the LNER and continued by BR, have shown their ability to sustain 80 mph on the level, while some large-wheeled express engines with less refined valve and front end design found it difficult to exceed 65 mph under similar conditions. The Maunsell S15 'fast-goods' 4-6-0s of the Southern, thanks to their more modern front end design, were more suitable to stand in as express engines at holiday periods than some earlier 'mixed-traffic' or 'express passenger' locomotives.

Below: Hawksworth Modified Hall No 7924 *Thornycroft Hall* **at Swindon shed 8 October 1950 two days after being built**
P M ALEXANDER

GREAT WESTERN RAILWAY

W Dean

No 36	1896	domed boiler, 2 inside cylinders	Heavy goods	

W Dean (boiler G J Churchward)

No 2601	1899	domeless boiler, 2 inside cylinders	Heavy goods	

G J Churchward (W Dean still nominally Locomotive Superintendent)

No 100	1902	domeless boiler, 2 outside cylinders	Express passenger	

G J Churchward

Saint class	1903	taper boiler, 2 outside cylinders	Express passenger	
Star class	1907	taper boiler, 4 cylinders	Express passenger	P

C B Collett

Castle class	1923	taper boiler, 4 cylinders	Express passenger	P
King class	1927	taper boiler, 4 cylinders	Express passenger	P
Hall class	1928	taper boiler, 2 outside cylinders	Mixed traffic	P
Grange class	1936	taper boiler, 2 outside cylinders	Mixed traffic	
Manor class	1938	taper boiler, 2 outside cylinders	Mixed traffic	P

F W Hawksworth

County class	1945	taper boiler, 2 outside cylinders	Mixed traffic	

Major rebuilds, G J Churchward
2-cylinder Atlantics rebuilt as Saint class 4-6-0s 1907-1912
4-cylinder Atlantic No 40 rebuilt as Star class 4-6-0 1909

Major rebuilds, C B Collett
Pacific No 111 *The Great Bear* rebuilt as Castle class 4-6-0 1924
No 2925 *Saint Martin* rebuilt as mixed-traffic engine (Hall class) 1924

LONDON AND NORTH WESTERN RAILWAY

F W Webb

1400 class	1902	4-cylinder compound	Mixed traffic

G Whale

Experiment class	1905	2 inside cylinders	Express passenger
'19 in Goods' (285) class		2 inside cylinders	Mixed traffic

C J Bowen Cooke

Prince	1911	2 inside cylinders	Express passenger
Claughton	1913	4 cylinders	Express passenger

Major rebuilds, C J Bowen Cooke
Experiment No 1361 *Prospero* rebuilt in 1915 with 4 cylinders and the Dendy Marshall valve gear

LANCASHIRE AND YORKSHIRE RAILWAY

G Hughes

1506 class	1908	4 cylinders	Express passenger

Major rebuild, G Hughes

1522	1920	1506 class rebuilt with superheater and piston valves. More built new 1923-1925 by the LMS	

CALEDONIAN RAILWAY

J F McIntosh

55 class	1902	2 inside cylinders	Mixed traffic (Oban line)
49/50	1903	2 inside cylinders	Express passenger
Cardean class	1906	2 inside cylinders	Express passenger
918 class	1906	2 inside cylinders	Express goods
908 class	1906	2 inside cylinders	Mixed traffic

W Pickersgill

60 class	1916	2 outside cylinders	Express passenger	
956 class	1921	3 cylinders	Express passenger	
191 class	1922	2 outside cylinders	Mixed traffic (Oban line)	

GLASGOW AND SOUTH WESTERN RAILWAY

J Manson
| 384 class | 1903 | 2 outside cylinders | Express passenger | |
| 128/129 | 1911 | 2 outside cylinders | Express passenger | |

THE HIGHLAND RAILWAY

David Jones
| 'Big Goods' class | 1894 | 2 outside cylinders | Fast goods | P |

P Drummond
| Castle class | 1900 | 2 outside cylinders | Express passenger | |

F G Smith
| River class | 1915 | 2 outside cylinders | Express passenger | |
| | | Rejected by Civil Engineer, sold to Caledonian | | |

C Cummings
| Clan class | 1918 | 2 outside cylinders | Express passenger | |
| Clan Goods class | 1918 | 2 outside cylinders | Fast goods | |

LONDON MIDLAND AND SCOTTISH RAILWAY

Sir Henry Fowler
| Royal Scot class | 1927 | 3 cylinders | Express passenger | |
| No 6399 *Fury* | 1929 | 3-cylinder compound, Schmidt-Henschel boiler experimental express locomotive | | |

Major rebuilds, Sir Henry Fowler
No 10456 Hughes 4-6-0 rebuilt in 1926 as a 4-cylinder compound
Patriot class, Claughtons replaced in 1930 with 3 cylinders, and larger boiler, the first contained some parts of the originals, later examples were new

Sir William Stanier
| Jubilee class | 1934 | 3 cylinders | Express passenger | P |
| Black Five class | 1934 | 2 outside cylinders | Mixed traffic | P |

Major rebuilds, Sir William Stanier
6170 *British Legion*	1936	No 6399 *Fury* rebuilt with conventional taper boiler and 3 simple cylinders		
5735/6	1942	Jubilees rebuilt with larger boiler and double chimney		
Converted Royal Scots	1943	Royal Scot rebuilt with boiler as above and improved valves and steam passages		P

H G Ivatt
| Rebuilt Patriots | 1946 | Patriots rebuilt with boiler as above | | |

NORTH EASTERN RAILWAY

Wilson Worsdell
| Class S | 1899 | 2 outside cylinders | Mixed traffic | |
| Class S1 | 1900 | 2 outside cylinders | Express passenger | |

Sir Vincent Raven
Class S2	1911	2 outside cylinders	Mixed traffic	
No 825	1913	Stumpf Uniflow	Mixed traffic	
Class S3	1919	3 cylinders	Mixed traffic	

GREAT EASTERN RAILWAY

S D Holden

1500 class	1911	2 inside cylinders	Express passenger	

GREAT CENTRAL RAILWAY

J G Robinson

Class 8	class	1902	2 outside cylinders	Mixed traffic
Class 8G	class	1903	2 outside cylinders	Express passenger
Class 8F	class	1906	2 outside cylinders	Express passenger
Class 8G	class	1906	2 outside cylinders	Fast goods
Class 1	class	1912	2 inside cylinders	Express passenger
Class 1A	class	1913	2 inside cylinders	Mixed traffic
Class 9P	class	1917	4 cylinders	Express passenger
Class 8N	class	1918	2 outside cylinders	Mixed traffic
Class 9Q	class	1921	4 cylinders	Mixed traffic

LONDON AND NORTH EASTERN RAILWAY

Sir Nigel Gresley

B17 class	1928	3 cylinders	Express passenger	

Major rebuilds, Sir Nigel Gresley

Class B12/3	1932	GER 1500 class rebuilt with larger boiler and improved valve gear and front end	P
Class B16/2	1937	NER S3 class rebuilt with modern front end and Gresley 2 and 1 valve gear	

Edward Thompson

B1 class	1942	2 outside cylinders	Mixed traffic	P

Major rebuilds, Edward Thompson

B3/3 No 6166/1497	1943	4-cylinder B3 rebuilt with two cylinders
B16/3 class	1944	B16 rebuilt with 3 sets of Walschaert's gear
B2 class	1945	B17 rebuilt with two cylinders

LONDON AND SOUTH WESTERN RAILWAY

Dugald Drummond

F13	1906	4 cylinders	Express passenger	
E14	1907	4 cylinders	Express passenger	
G14	1908	4 cylinders	Express passenger	
P14	1910	4 cylinders	Express passenger	
T14	1911	4 cylinders	Express passenger	

Robert Urie

H15	1914	2 outside cylinders	Mixed traffic	
N15	1918	2 outside cylinders	Express passenger	
S15	1920	2 outside cylinders	Fast goods	

R E L Maunsell

N15 (King Arthur)	1925	2 outside cylinders	Express passenger	P
Lord Nelson	1926	4 cylinders	Express passenger	P
S15	1927	2 outside cylinders	Fast goods	P

Major rebuilds, R E L Maunsell
F13s Nos 331-335 rebuilt as 2-cylinder H15s class in 1924
N15X class Former LB&SCR 4-6-4 tank engines rebuilt as 4-6-0s in 1934/6

BRITISH RAILWAYS

73 class	1951	2 outside cylinders	Mixed traffic	P
75 class	1951	2 outside cylinders	Mixed traffic	P